Academia Isa San Juan

Unit 1 - Present continuous (I am doing) - lesson

Study this example situation:

Sarah is in her car. She is on her way to work.
She **is driving** to work.

This means: she is driving *now*, at the time of speaking.
The action is not finished.

Am/is/are + -ing is the *present continuous:*

	I	am	(= I'm)
he/she/it		is	(= he's etc.)
we/you/they		are	(= we're etc.)

driving
working
doing etc.

I am doing something = I'm in the middle of doing it; I've started doing it and I haven't finished yet:

- ☐ Please don't make so much noise. **I'm trying** to work. (*not* I try)
- ☐ 'Where's Mark?' '**He's having** a shower.' (*not* He has a shower)
- ☐ Let's go out now. It **isn't raining** any more. (*not* It doesn't rain)
- ☐ *(at a party)* Hello, Jane. **Are** you **enjoying** the party? (*not* Do you enjoy)
- ☐ What's all that noise? What's **going** on? (= What's happening?)

The action is not necessarily happening at the time of speaking. For example:

Steve is talking to a friend on the phone. He says:

> I'm reading a really good book at the moment.
> It's about a man who ...

Steve is not reading the book at the time of speaking.
He means that he has started it, but has not finished it yet.
He is in the middle of reading it.

Some more examples:

- ☐ Kate wants to work in Italy, so she's **learning** Italian. (but perhaps she isn't learning Italian at the time of speaking)
- ☐ Some friends of mine **are building** their own house. They hope to finish it next summer.

You can use the present continuous with **today / this week / this year** etc. (periods around now):

- ☐ A: You're **working** hard **today**. (*not* You work hard today)
  B: Yes, I have a lot to do.
- ☐ The company I work for **isn't doing** so well **this year**.

We use the present continuous when we talk about changes happening around now, especially with these verbs:

get   change   become   increase   rise   fall   grow   improve   begin   start

- ☐ **Is** your English **getting** better? (*not* Does your English get better)
- ☐ The population of the world **is increasing** very fast. (*not* increases)
- ☐ At first I didn't like my job, but **I'm beginning** to enjoy it now. (*not* I begin)

Unit 1 - Present continuous (I am doing) - exercises

1.1 Complete the sentences with the following verbs in the correct form:

get   happen   ~~look~~   lose   make   start   stay   try   ~~work~~

1 'You __'re working__ hard today.'   'Yes, I have a lot to do.'
2 I .... for Christine. Do you know where she is?
3 It .... dark. Shall I turn on the light?
4 They don't have anywhere to live at the moment. They .... with friends until they find somewhere.
5 Things are not so good at work. The company .... money.
6 Have you got an umbrella? It .... to rain.
7 You .... a lot of noise. Can you be quieter? I .... to concentrate.
8 Why are all these people here? What .... ?

1.2 Put the verb into the correct form. Sometimes you need the negative (I'm not doing etc.).

1 Please don't make so much noise. I __'m trying__ (try) to work.
2 Let's go out now. It __isn't raining__ (rain) any more.
3 You can turn off the radio. I .... (listen) to it.
4 Kate phoned me last night. She's on holiday in France. She .... (have) a great time and doesn't want to come back.
5 I want to lose weight, so this week I .... (eat) lunch.
6 Andrew has just started evening classes. He .... (learn) German.
7 Paul and Sally have had an argument. They .... (speak) to each other.
8 I .... (get) tired. I need a rest.
9 Tim .... (work) this week. He's on holiday.

1.3 Complete the conversations.

1 A: I saw Brian a few days ago.
  B: Oh, did you? __What's he doing__ these days? (what / he / do)
  A: He's at university.
  B: .... ? (what / he / study)
  A: Psychology.
  B: .... it? (he / enjoy)
  A: Yes, he says it's a very good course.

2 A: Hi, Liz. How .... in your new job? (you / get on)
  B: Not bad. It wasn't so good at first, but .... better now. (things / get)
  A: What about Jonathan? Is he OK?
  B: Yes, but .... his work at the moment. (he / not / enjoy) He's been in the same job for a long time and .... to get bored with it. (he / begin)

1.4 Complete the sentences using the following verbs:

begin   change   get   ~~increase~~   rise

1 The population of the world __is increasing__ very fast.
2 The world .... Things never stay the same.
3 The situation is already bad and it .... worse.
4 The cost of living .... Every year things are more expensive.
5 The weather .... to improve. The rain has stopped, and the wind isn't as strong.

Unit 2 - Present simple (I do) - lesson

Study this example situation:

Alex is a bus driver, but now he is in bed asleep.
He is not driving a bus. (He is asleep.)
but He **drives** a bus. (He is a bus driver.)
Drive(s)/work(s)/do(es) etc. is the *present simple*:

I/we/you/they **drive/work/do** etc.
he/she/it **drives/works/does** etc.

We use the present simple to talk about things in general. We use it to say that something happens all the time or repeatedly, or that something is true in general:
- □ Nurses **look** after patients in hospitals.
- □ I usually **go** away at weekends.
- □ The earth **goes** round the sun.
- □ The café **opens** at 7.30 in the morning.

Remember:

I work … *but* He **works** …   They **teach** … *but* My sister **teaches** …

For spelling (**-s** or **-es**), see Appendix 6.

We use **do/does** to make questions and negative sentences:

do does	I/we/you/they he/she/it	work? drive? do?	I/we/you/they he/she/it	don't doesn't	work drive do

- □ I come from Canada. Where **do** you **come** from?
- □ I **don't go** away very often.
- □ What **does** this word **mean**? (*not* What means this word?)
- □ Rice **doesn't grow** in cold climates.

In the following examples, do is also the main verb (do you **do** / doesn't **do** etc.):
- □ 'What **do** you **do**?' 'I work in a shop.'
- □ He's always so lazy. He **doesn't do** anything to help.

We use the present simple to say how often we do things:
- □ I **get** up at 8 o'clock **every morning**.
- □ **How often** do you **go** to the dentist?
- □ Julie **doesn't drink** tea **very often**.
- □ Robert usually **goes** away **two or three times a year**.

I promise / I apologise etc.

Sometimes we do things by saying something. For example, when you *promise* to do something, you can say 'I promise …'; when you *suggest* something, you can say 'I suggest …':
- □ I **promise** I won't be late. (*not* I'm promising)
- □ 'What do you **suggest** I do?' 'I **suggest** that you …'

In the same way we say: I **apologise** … / I **advise** … / I **insist** … / I **agree** … / I **refuse** … etc.

Unit 2 - Present simple (I do) - exercises

2.1 Complete the sentences using the following verbs:

cause(s) connect(s) drink(s) live(s) open(s) ~~speak(s)~~ take(s)

1 Tanya __speaks__ German very well.
2 I don't often .... coffee.
3 The swimming pool .... at 7.30 every morning.
4 Bad driving .... many accidents.
5 My parents .... in a very small flat.
6 The Olympic Games .... place every four years.
7 The Panama Canal .... the Atlantic and Pacific oceans.

2.2 Put the verb into the correct form.

1 Julie __doesn't drink__ (not / drink) tea very often.
2 What time .... (the banks / close) here?
3 I've got a computer, but I .... (not / use) it much.
4 'Where .... (Martin / come) from?' 'He's Scottish.'
5 'What .... (you / do)?' 'I'm an electrician.'
6 It .... (take) me an hour to get to work. How long .... (it / take) you?
7 Look at this sentence. What .... (this word / mean)?
8 David isn't very fit. He .... (not / do) any sport.

2.3 Use the following verbs to complete the sentences. Sometimes you need the negative:

believe ~~eat~~ flow ~~go~~ ~~grow~~ make rise tell translate

1 The earth __goes__ round the sun.
2 Rice __doesn't grow__ in Britain.
3 The sun .... in the east.
4 Bees .... honey.
5 Vegetarians .... meat.
6 An atheist .... in God.
7 An interpreter .... from one language into another.
8 Liars are people who .... the truth.
9 The River Amazon .... into the Atlantic Ocean.

2.4 You ask Liz questions about herself and her family. Write the questions.

1 You know that Liz plays tennis. You want to know how often. Ask her.
How often __do you play tennis__ ?
2 Perhaps Liz's sister plays tennis too. You want to know. Ask Liz.
.... your sister ?
3 You know that Liz reads a newspaper every day. You want to know which one. Ask her.
.... ?
4 You know that Liz's brother works. You want to know what he does. Ask Liz.
.... ?
5 You know that Liz goes to the cinema a lot. You want to know how often. Ask her.
.... ?
6 You don't know where Liz's grandparents live. You want to know. Ask Liz.
.... ?

2.5 Complete using the following:

I apologise I insist I promise I recommend ~~I suggest~~

1 It's a nice day. __I suggest__ we go out for a walk.
2 I won't tell anybody what you said. ....
3 (in a restaurant) You must let me pay for the meal. ....
4 .... for what I did. It won't happen again.
5 The new restaurant in Hill Street is very good. .... it.

Unit 3 - Present continuous and present simple (1) - lesson

Compare:

Present continuous (**I am doing**)	*Present simple* (**I do**)
We use the continuous for things happening at or around the time of speaking. The action is not complete.	We use the simple for things in general or things that happen repeatedly.

I am doing	◄—————— I do ——————►
past *now* *future*	*past* *now* *future*

□ The water **is boiling**. Can you turn it off?	□ Water **boils** at 100 degrees Celsius.
□ Listen to those people. What language **are** they **speaking**?	□ Excuse me, **do** you **speak** English?
□ Let's go out. It **isn't raining** now.	□ It **doesn't rain** very much in summer.
□ 'I'm busy.' 'What **are** you **doing**?'	□ What **do** you usually **do** at weekends?
□ I'**m getting** hungry. Let's go and eat.	□ I always **get** hungry in the afternoon.
□ Kate wants to work in Italy, so she's **learning** Italian.	□ Most people **learn** to swim when they are children.
□ The population of the world **is increasing** very fast.	□ Every day the population of the world **increases** by about 200,000 people.

We use the continuous for *temporary* situations:	We use the simple for *permanent* situations:
□ I'**m living** with some friends until I find a place of my own.	□ My parents **live** in London. They have lived there all their lives.
□ A: You'**re working** hard today. B: Yes, I have a lot to do.	□ John isn't lazy. He **works** hard most of the time.
See Unit 1 for more information.	See Unit 2 for more information.

I always do and **I'm always doing**

I always do (something) = I do it every time:
   □ I **always go** to work by car. (*not* I'm always going)

'**I'm always doing** something' has a different meaning. For example:

I've lost my pen again. I'm **always losing** things.

I'**m always losing** things = I lose things very often, perhaps too often, or more often than normal.

Two more examples:
   □ You'**re always watching** television. You should do something more active. (= You watch television too often)
   □ Tim is never satisfied. He'**s always complaining**. (= He complains too much)

10

Unit 3 - Present continuous and present simple (1) - exercises

3.1 Are the underlined verbs right or wrong? Correct them where necessary.

1 Water boils at 100 degrees Celsius.   OK
2 The water boils. Can you turn it off?   *is boiling*
3 Look! That man tries to open the door of your car.
4 Can you hear those people? What do they talk about?
5 The moon goes round the earth in about 27 days.
6 I must go now. It gets late.
7 I usually go to work by car.
8 'Hurry up! It's time to leave.' 'OK, I come.'
9 I hear you've got a new job. How do you get on?
10 Paul is never late. He's always getting to work on time.
11 They don't get on well. They're always arguing.

3.2 Put the verb into the correct form, present continuous or present simple.

1 Let's go out. It ___isn't raining___ (not / rain) now.
2 Julia is very good at languages. She ___speaks___ (speak) four languages very well.
3 Hurry up! Everybody _____ (wait) for you.
4 '_____ (you / listen) to the radio?' 'No, you can turn it off.'
5 '_____ (you / listen) to the radio every day?' 'No, just occasionally.'
6 The River Nile _____ (flow) into the Mediterranean.
7 The river _____ (flow) very fast today – much faster than usual.
8 We usually _____ (grow) vegetables in our garden, but this year we _____ (not / grow) any.
9 A: How's your English?
   B: Not bad. I think it _____ (improve) slowly.
10 Rachel is in London at the moment. She _____ (stay) at the Park Hotel.
   She always _____ (stay) there when she's in London.
11 Can we stop walking soon? I _____ (start) to feel tired.
12 A: Can you drive?
   B: I _____ (learn). My father _____ (teach) me.
13 Normally I _____ (finish) work at five, but this week I _____ (work) until six to earn a little more money.
14 My parents _____ (live) in Manchester. They were born there and have never lived anywhere else. Where _____ (your parents / live)?
15 Sonia _____ (look) for a place to live. She _____ (stay) with her sister until she finds somewhere.
16 A: What _____ (your brother / do)?
   B: He's an architect, but he _____ (not / work) at the moment.
17 *(at a party)* I usually _____ (enjoy) parties, but I _____ (not / enjoy) this one very much.

3.3 Finish B's sentences. Use always -ing.

1 A: I've lost my pen again.
   B: Not again! *You're always losing your pen* .
2 A: The car has broken down again.
   B: That car is useless. It _____ .
3 A: Look! You've made the same mistake again.
   B: Oh no, not again! I _____ .
4 A: Oh, I've forgotten my glasses again.
   B: Typical! _____ .

Unit 4 - Present continuous and present simple (2) - lesson

We use continuous forms for actions and happenings that have started but not finished (they **are eating** / it **is raining** etc.). Some verbs (for example, **know** and **like**) are not normally used in this way. We don't say 'I am knowing' or 'they are liking'; we say '**I know**', 'they **like**'.

The following verbs are not normally used in the present continuous:

like love hate want need prefer
know realise suppose mean understand believe remember
belong fit contain consist seem

- ☐ I'm hungry. I **want** something to eat. (*not* I'm wanting)
- ☐ Do you **understand** what I **mean**?
- ☐ Ann **doesn't seem** very happy at the moment.

Think

When **think** means 'believe' or 'have an opinion', we do not use the continuous:
- ☐ I **think** Mary is Canadian, but I'm not sure. (*not* I'm thinking)
- ☐ What **do** you **think** about my plan? (= What is your opinion?)

When **think** means 'consider', the continuous is possible:
- ☐ I'm **thinking** about what happened. I often **think** about it.
- ☐ Nicky **is thinking** of giving up her job. (= she is considering it)

He is selfish and He is being selfish

He's **being** = He's behaving / He's acting. Compare:
- ☐ I can't understand why he's **being** so selfish. He isn't usually like that.
  (being selfish = behaving selfishly at the moment)
- ☐ He never thinks about other people. He **is** very selfish. (*not* He is being)
  (= He is selfish generally, not only at the moment)

We use **am/is/are being** to say how somebody is *behaving*. It is not usually possible in other sentences:
- ☐ It's hot today. (*not* It is being hot)
- ☐ Sarah **is** very tired. (*not* is being tired)

See hear smell taste

We normally use the present simple (not continuous) with these verbs:
- ☐ Do you **see** that man over there? (*not* Are you seeing)
- ☐ This room **smells**. Let's open a window.

We often use **can** + see/hear/smell/taste:
- ☐ I **can hear** a strange noise. **Can** you **hear** it?

Look feel

You can use the present simple or continuous to say how somebody looks or feels now:
- ☐ You **look** well today. *or* You're **looking** well today.
- ☐ How **do** you **feel** now? *or* How **are** you **feeling** now?

but
- ☐ I usually **feel** tired in the morning. (*not* I'm usually feeling)

Unit 4 - Present continuous and present simple (2) - exercises

4.1 Are the <u>underlined</u> verbs right or wrong? Correct them where necessary.

1 Nicky <u>is thinking</u> of giving up her job.   OK
2 <u>Are</u> you <u>believing</u> in God?
3 <u>I'm feeling</u> hungry. Is there anything to eat?
4 This sauce is great. It<u>'s tasting</u> really good.
5 <u>I'm thinking</u> this is your key. Am I right?

4.2 Use the words in brackets to make sentences. (You should also study Unit 3 before you do this exercise.)

1	2
(you / not / seem / very happy today) You don't seem very happy today.	(what / you / do?) Be quiet! (I / think)
3 (who / this umbrella / belong to?) I have no idea.	4 (the dinner / smell / good)
5 Excuse me. (anybody / sit / there?) No, it's free.	6 (these gloves / not / fit / me) They're too small.

4.3 Put the verb into the correct form, present continuous or present simple.

1 Are you hungry? ___Do you want___ (you / want) something to eat?
2 Don't put the dictionary away. I _____ (use) it.
3 Don't put the dictionary away. I _____ (need) it.
4 Who is that man? What _____ (he / want)?
5 Who is that man? Why _____ (he / look) at us?
6 Alan says he's 80 years old, but nobody _____ (believe) him.
7 She told me her name, but I _____ (not / remember) it now.
8 I _____ (think) of selling my car. Would you be interested in buying it?
9 I _____ (think) you should sell your car. You _____ (not / use) it very often.
10 Air _____ (consist) mainly of nitrogen and oxygen.

4.4 Complete the sentences using the most suitable form of be. Sometimes you must use the simple (am/is/are) and sometimes the continuous is more suitable (am/is/are being).

1 I can't understand why __he's being__ so selfish. He isn't usually like that.
2 Sarah _____ very nice to me at the moment. I wonder why.
3 You'll like Debbie when you meet her. She _____ very nice.
4 You're usually very patient, so why _____ so unreasonable about waiting ten more minutes?
5 Why isn't Steve at work today? _____ ill?

9

Unit 5 - Past simple (I did) - lesson

Study this example:

Wolfgang Amadeus Mozart was an Austrian musician and composer. He **lived** from 1756 to 1791. He **started** composing at the age of five and **wrote** more than 600 pieces of music. He **was** only 35 years old when he **died**.

Lived/started/wrote/was/died are all *past simple*.

Very often the past simple ends in **-ed** (*regular* verbs):
- ☐ I work in a travel agency now. Before that **I worked** in a department store.
- ☐ We **invited** them to our party, but they **decided** not to come.
- ☐ The police **stopped** me on my way home last night.
- ☐ Laura **passed** her examination because she **studied** very hard.

For spelling (stopped, studied etc.), see Appendix 6.

But many verbs are *irregular*. The past simple does *not* end in **-ed**. For example:

write	→	**wrote**	☐ Mozart **wrote** more than 600 pieces of music.
see	→	**saw**	☐ We **saw** Rose in town a few days ago.
go	→	**went**	☐ I **went** to the cinema three times last week.
shut	→	**shut**	☐ It was cold, so **I shut** the window.

For a list of irregular verbs, see Appendix 1.

In questions and negatives we use **did/didn't** + *infinitive* (enjoy/see/go etc.):

I	enjoyed
she	saw
they	went

did	you	enjoy?
	she	see?
	they	go?

I		enjoy
she	didn't	see
they		go

- ☐ A: **Did** you **go** out last night?
  B: Yes, I **went** to the cinema, but I **didn't enjoy** the film much.
- ☐ 'When **did** Mr Thomas **die**?' 'About ten years ago.'
- ☐ They **didn't invite** her to the party, so she **didn't go**.
- ☐ '**Did** you **have** time to write the letter?' 'No, I **didn't**.'

In the following examples, **do** is the main verb in the sentence (**did ... do / didn't do**):
- ☐ What **did** you **do** at the weekend? (*not* What did you at the weekend?)
- ☐ I **didn't do** anything. (*not* I didn't anything)

The past of be (**am/is/are**) is **was/were**:

| I/he/she/it | was/wasn't |
| we/you/they | were/weren't |

| was | I/he/she/it? |
| were | we/you/they? |

Note that we do not use **did** in negatives and questions with **was/were**:
- ☐ I **was** angry because they **were** late.
- ☐ **Was** the weather good when you **were** on holiday?
- ☐ They **weren't** able to come because they **were** so busy.
- ☐ Did you go out last night or **were** you too tired?

Unit 5 - Past simple (I did) - exercises

5.1 Read what Laura says about a typical working day:

> I usually get up at 7 o'clock and have a big breakfast. I walk to work, which takes me about half an hour. I start work at 8.45. I never have lunch. I finish work at 5 o'clock. I'm always tired when I get home. I usually cook a meal in the evening. I don't usually go out. I go to bed at about 11 o'clock, and I always sleep well.

Laura

Yesterday was a typical working day for Laura. Write what she did or didn't do yesterday.

1 _She got up at 7 o'clock._
2 She _____ a big breakfast.
3 She _____ .
4 It _____ to get to work.
5 _____ at 8.45.
6 _____ lunch.
7 _____ at 5 o'clock.
8 _____ tired when _____ home.
9 _____ a meal yesterday evening.
10 _____ out yesterday evening.
11 _____ at 11 o'clock.
12 _____ well last night.

5.2 Complete the sentences using the following verbs in the correct form:

buy   catch   cost   fall   hurt   sell   spend   teach   throw   ~~write~~

1 Mozart _wrote_ more than 600 pieces of music.
2 'How did you learn to drive?' 'My father _____ me.'
3 We couldn't afford to keep our car, so we _____ it.
4 Dave _____ down the stairs this morning and _____ his leg.
5 Jim _____ the ball to Sue, who _____ it.
6 Ann _____ a lot of money yesterday. She _____ a dress which _____ £100.

5.3 You ask James about his holiday. Write your questions.
   Hi. How are things?
            Fine, thanks. I've just had a great holiday.
1 Where _did you go_ ?
            To the U.S. We went on a trip from San Francisco to Denver.
2 How _____ ? By car?
            Yes, we hired a car in San Francisco.
3 It's a long way to drive. How long _____ ?
            Two weeks.
4 Where _____ ? In hotels?
            Yes, small hotels or motels.
5 _____ ?
            Yes, but it was very hot – sometimes too hot.
6 _____ the Grand Canyon?
            Of course. It was wonderful.

5.4 Complete the sentences. Put the verb into the correct form, positive or negative.
1 It was warm, so I _took_ off my coat. (take)
2 The film wasn't very good. I _didn't enjoy_ it very much. (enjoy)
3 I knew Sarah was very busy, so I _____ her. (disturb)
4 I was very tired, so I _____ the party early. (leave)
5 The bed was very uncomfortable. I _____ very well. (sleep)
6 The window was open and a bird _____ into the room. (fly)
7 The hotel wasn't very expensive. It _____ very much. (cost)
8 I was in a hurry, so I _____ time to phone you. (have)
9 It was hard carrying the bags. They _____ very heavy. (be)

11

Unit 6 - Past continuous (I was doing) - lesson

Study this example situation:

Yesterday Karen and Jim played tennis. They began at 10 o'clock and finished at 11.30.
So, at 10.30 they **were playing** tennis.

They **were playing** = they were in the middle of playing. They had not finished playing.

Was/were -ing is the *past continuous*:

I/he/she/it	**was**	playing
we/you/they	**were**	doing
		working etc.

I **was doing** something = I was in the middle of doing something at a certain time. The action or situation had already started before this time, but had not finished:

I started doing	**I was doing**	**I finished doing**	
past		*past*	*now*

- ☐ This time last year I **was living** in Brazil.
- ☐ What **were** you **doing** at 10 o'clock last night?
- ☐ I waved to Helen, but she **wasn't looking**.

Compare the *past continuous* (I **was doing**) and *past simple* (I **did**):

Past continuous (in the middle of an action)	*Past simple* (complete action)
☐ I **was walking** home when I met Dave. (in the middle of an action)	☐ I **walked** home after the party last night. (= all the way, completely)
☐ Kate **was watching** television when we arrived.	☐ Kate **watched** television a lot when she was ill last year.

We often use the past simple and the past continuous together to say that something happened in the middle of something else:

- ☐ Matt **phoned** while we **were having** dinner.
- ☐ It **was raining** when I **got** up.
- ☐ I **saw** you in the park yesterday. You **were sitting** on the grass and **reading** a book.
- ☐ I **hurt** my back while I **was working** in the garden.

But we use the past simple to say that one thing happened after another:

- ☐ I **was walking** along the road when I **saw** Dave. So I **stopped**, and we **had** a chat.

Compare:

☐ When Karen arrived, we **were having** dinner. (= we had already started before she arrived)	☐ When Karen arrived, we **had** dinner. (= Karen arrived, and then we had dinner)

Some verbs (for example, **know** and **want**) are not normally used in the continuous (see Unit 4A):

- ☐ We were good friends. We **knew** each other well. (*not* We were knowing)
- ☐ I was enjoying the party, but Chris **wanted** to go home. (*not* was wanting)

Unit 6 - Past continuous (I was doing) - exercises

6.1 What were you doing at these times? Write sentences as in the examples. The past continuous is not always necessary (see the second example).

1 (at 8 o'clock yesterday evening) _I was having dinner._
2 (at 5 o'clock last Monday) _I was on a bus on my way home._
3 (at 10.15 yesterday morning) ....
4 (at 4.30 this morning) ....
5 (at 7.45 yesterday evening) ....
6 (half an hour ago) ....

6.2 Use your own ideas to complete the sentences. Use the past continuous.

1 Matt phoned while we _were having dinner_ .
2 The doorbell rang while I ....
3 We saw an accident while we ....
4 Ann fell asleep while she ....
5 The television was on, but nobody ....

6.3 Put the verb into the correct form, past continuous or past simple.

I _saw_ (see) Sue in town yesterday, but she .... (not / see) me. She .... (look) the other way.

I .... (meet) Tom and Jane at the airport a few weeks ago. They .... (go) to Paris and I .... (go) to Rome. We .... (have) a chat while we .... (wait) for our flights.

I .... (cycle) home yesterday when a man .... (step) out into the road in front of me. I .... (go) quite fast, but luckily I .... (manage) to stop in time and .... (not / hit) him.

6.4 Put the verb into the correct form, past continuous or past simple.

1 Jenny _was waiting_ (wait) for me when I _arrived_ (arrive).
2 'What .... (you / do) at this time yesterday?' 'I was asleep.'
3 '.. (you / go) out last night?' 'No, I was too tired.'
4 How fast .... (you / drive) when the accident .... (happen)?
5 Sam .... (take) a photograph of me while I .... (not / look).
6 We were in a very difficult position. We .... (not / know) what to do.
7 I haven't seen Alan for ages. When I last .... (see) him, he .... (try) to find a job.
8 I .... (walk) along the street when suddenly I .... (hear) footsteps behind me. Somebody .... (follow) me. I was scared and I .... (start) to run.
9 When I was young, I .... (want) to be a pilot.
10 Last night I .... (drop) a plate when I .... (do) the washing up. Fortunately it .... (not / break).

Unit 7 - Present perfect 1 (I have done) - lesson

Study this example situation:

Tom is looking for his key. He can't find it.
He **has lost** his key.

He **has lost** his key = He lost it recently, and he still doesn't have it.

Have/has lost is the *present perfect simple*:

I/we/they/you	**have**	(= I've etc.)	finished lost
he/she/it	**has**	(= he's etc.)	done been etc.

The present perfect simple is **have/has** + *past participle*. The past participle often ends in -ed (finished/decided etc.), but many important verbs are *irregular* (**lost/done/written** etc.).

For a list of irregular verbs, see Appendix 1.

When we say that 'something **has happened**', this is usually new information:
- □ Ow! **I've cut** my finger.
- □ The road is closed. There's **been** (there **has** been) an accident.
- □ (*from the news*) Police **have arrested** two men in connection with the robbery.

When we use the present perfect, there is a connection with *now*. The action in the past has a result *now*:
- □ 'Where's your key?' 'I don't know. **I've lost** it.' (= I don't have it *now*)
- □ He told me his name, but **I've forgotten** it. (= I can't remember it *now*)
- □ 'Is Sally here?' 'No, **she's gone** out.' (= she is out *now*)
- □ I can't find my bag. **Have you seen** it? (= Do you know where it is *now*?)

You can use the present perfect with **just, already** and **yet**.

Just = a short time ago:
- □ 'Are you hungry?' 'No, **I've just had** lunch.'
- □ Hello. **Have you just arrived**?

We use **already** to say that something happened sooner than expected:
- □ 'Don't forget to send the letter.' '**I've already sent** it.'
- □ 'What time is Mark leaving?' '**He's already gone**.'

Yet = until now. **Yet** shows that the speaker is expecting something to happen. Use **yet** only in questions and negative sentences:
- □ **Has it stopped** raining yet?
- □ I've written the letter, but I **haven't sent** it yet.

Note the difference between **gone** (to) and **been** (to):
- □ Jim is on holiday. He **has gone to** Italy. (= he is there now or on his way there)
- □ Jane is back home now. She **has been to** Italy. (= she has now come back)

Unit 7 - Present perfect 1 (I have done) - exercises

7.1 Read the situations and write sentences. Use the following verbs:

arrive   break   fall   go up   grow   improve   ~~lose~~

1 Tom is looking for his key. He can't find it.   He has lost his key.
2 Margaret can't walk and her leg is in plaster.   She ....
3 Last week the bus fare was 80 pence. Now it is 90. The bus fare ....
4 Maria's English wasn't very good. Now it is better. Her English ....
5 Dan didn't have a beard before. Now he has a beard. He ....
6 This morning I was expecting a letter. Now I have it. The letter ....
7 The temperature was 20 degrees. Now it is only 12. The ....

7.2 Complete B's sentences. Use the verb in brackets + just/already/yet.

A

1 Would you like something to eat?

2 Do you know where Julia is?

3 What time is David leaving?

4 What's in the newspaper today?

5 Is Sue coming to the cinema with us?

6 Are your friends here yet?

7 What does Tim think about your plan?

B

1 No, thanks. I've just had lunch.
(I / just / have / lunch)

2 Yes, ...
(I / just / see / her)

3 ....
(he / already / leave)

4 I don't know. ....
(I / not / read / it yet)

5 No, ...
(she / already / see / the film)

6 Yes, ...
(they / just / arrive)

7 ....
(we / not / tell / him yet)

7.3 Read the situations and write sentences with **just, already** or **yet**.

1 After lunch you go to see a friend at her house. She says, 'Would you like something to eat?'
  You say: No thank you. I've just had lunch . (have lunch)
2 Joe goes out. Five minutes later, the phone rings and the caller says, 'Can I speak to Joe?'
  You say: I'm afraid .... (go out)
3 You are eating in a restaurant. The waiter thinks you have finished and starts to take your
  plate away. You say: Wait a minute! .... (not / finish)
4 You are going to a restaurant tonight. You phone to reserve a table. Later your friend says,
  'Shall I phone to reserve a table.' You say: No, ... (do it)
5 You know that a friend of yours is looking for a place to live. Perhaps she has been successful.
  Ask her. You say: .... ? (find)
6 You are still thinking about where to go for your holiday. A friend asks, 'Where are you going
  for your holiday?' You say: .... (not /decide)
7 Linda went to the bank, but a few minutes ago she returned. Somebody asks, 'Is Linda still at
  the bank?' You say: No, ... (come back)

7.4 Put in **been** or **gone**.

1 Jim is on holiday. He's gone to Italy.
2 Hello! I've just .... to the shops. I've bought lots of things.
3 Alice isn't here at the moment. She's .... to the shop to get a newspaper.
4 Tom has .... out. He'll be back in about an hour.
5 'Are you going to the bank?' 'No, I've already .... to the bank.'

Unit 8 - Present perfect 2 (I have done) - lesson

Study this example conversation:

DAVE: **Have** you **travelled** a lot, Jane?
JANE: Yes, I've **been** to lots of places.
DAVE: Really? **Have** you ever **been** to China?
JANE: Yes, I've **been** to China twice.
DAVE: What about India?
JANE: No, I **haven't been** to India.

Jane's life
(a period until now)

past   now

When we talk about a period of time that continues from the past until now, we use the *present perfect* (**have been / have travelled** etc.). Here, Dave and Jane are talking about the places Jane has visited in her life (which is a period that continues until now).

Some more examples:
- **Have** you ever **eaten** caviar? (in your life)
- We've never **had** a car.
- '**Have** you **read** *Hamlet?*' 'No, I **haven't read** any of Shakespeare's plays.'
- Susan really loves that film. She's **seen** it eight times!
- What a boring film! It's the most boring film I've **ever seen**.

Been (to) = visited:
- I've never **been** to China. Have you **been** there?

In the following examples too, the speakers are talking about a period that continues until now (**recently / in the last few days / so far / since breakfast** etc.):
- **Have** you **heard** from Brian **recently**?
- I've **met** a lot of people **in the last few days**.
- Everything is going well. We **haven't had** any problems **so far**.
- I'm hungry. I **haven't eaten** anything **since breakfast**. (= from breakfast until now)
- It's good to see you again. We **haven't seen** each other **for a long time**.

recently
in the last few days
since breakfast

past   now

We use the present perfect with **today / this evening / this year** etc. when these periods are not finished at the time of speaking (see also Unit 14B):
- I've **drunk** four cups of coffee **today**.
- **Have** you **had** a holiday **this year** (yet)?
- I **haven't seen** Tom **this morning**. Have you?
- Rob **hasn't studied** very hard **this term**.

today

past   now

We say: It's the (first) time something **has happened**. For example:
- Don is having a driving lesson. It's his first one.
  It's the first time he **has driven** a car. (*not* drives)
- or He **has never driven** a car before.
- Sarah has lost her passport again. This is the second time this **has happened**. (*not* happens)
- Bill is phoning his girlfriend again. That's the third time he's **phoned** her **this evening**.

This is the first time I've **driven** a car.

Unit 8 - Present perfect 2 (I have done) - exercises

8.1 You are asking people questions about things they have done. Make questions with **ever** using the words in brackets.

1 (ride / horse?) _Have you ever ridden a horse?_
2 (be / California?) Have _____
3 (run / marathon?) _____
4 (speak / famous person?) _____
5 (most beautiful place / visit?) What's _____

8.2 Complete B's answers. Some sentences are positive and some negative. Use the following verbs:

be   be   eat   happen   have   ~~meet~~   play   read   see   see   try

	A	B
1	What's Mark's sister like?	I've no idea. _I've never met_ her.
2	How is Diane these days?	I don't know. I _____ her recently.
3	Are you hungry?	Yes. I _____ much today.
4	Can you play chess?	Yes, but _____ for ages.
5	Are you enjoying your holiday?	Yes, it's the best holiday _____ for a long time.
6	What's that book like?	I don't know. _____ it.
7	Is Brussels an interesting place?	I've no idea. _____ there.
8	Mike was late for work again today.	Again? He _____ late every day this week.
9	Do you like caviar?	I don't know. _____ it.
10	I hear your car broke down again yesterday.	Yes, it's the second time _____ this week.
11	Who's that woman by the door?	I don't know. _____ her before.

8.3 Complete the sentences using **today / this year / this term** etc.

1 I saw Tom yesterday, but _I haven't seen him today_ .
3 I read a newspaper yesterday, but I _____ today.
4 Last year the company made a profit, but this year _____ .
4 Tracy worked hard at school last term, but _____ .
5 It snowed a lot last winter, but _____ .
6 Our football team won a lot of games last season, but we _____ .

8.4 Read the situations and write sentences as shown in the example.

1 Jack is driving a car, but he's very nervous and not sure what to do.
You ask: _Have you driven a car before?_
He says: _No, this is the first time I've driven a car._
2 Ben is playing tennis. He's not good at it and he doesn't know the rules.
You ask: Have _____
He says: No, this is the first _____
3 Sue is riding a horse. She doesn't look very confident or comfortable.
You ask: _____
She says: _____
4 Maria is in London. She has just arrived and it's very new for her.
You ask: _____
She says: _____

Unit 9 - Present perfect continuous (I have been doing) - lesson

It has been raining

Study this example situation:

Is it raining?
No, but the ground is wet.

It has been raining.

Have/has been -ing is the *present perfect continuous*:

I/we/they/you	**have**	(= I've etc.)	**been**	doing
he/she/it	**has**	(= he's etc.)		waiting
				playing etc.

We use the present perfect continuous for an activity that has recently stopped or just stopped. There is a connection with *now*:

☐ You're out of breath. **Have you been running?** (= you're out of breath *now*)
☐ Paul is very tired. He's **been working** very hard. (= he's tired *now*)
☐ Why are your clothes so dirty? What **have you been doing**?
☐ **I've been talking** to Amanda about the problem and she agrees with me.
☐ Where have you been? **I've been looking** for you everywhere.

It has been raining for two hours.

Study this example situation:

It began raining two hours ago and it is still raining.

How long **has it been raining**?
It **has been raining** for two hours.

We use the present perfect continuous in this way with **how long, for** ... and **since** ... . The activity is still happening (as in this example) or has just stopped.

☐ **How long have** you **been learning** English? (= you're still learning English)
☐ Tim is still watching television. He's **been watching** television **all day**.
☐ Where have you been? **I've been looking** for you **for the last half hour**.
☐ Chris **hasn't been feeling** well **recently**.

You can use the present prefect continuous for actions repeated over a period of time:

☐ Debbie is a very good tennis player. She's **been playing since she was eight**.
☐ Every morning they meet in the same café. They've **been going there for years**.

Compare **I am doing** (see Unit 1) and **I have been doing**:

I am doing *present continuous*	I have been doing *present perfect continuous*
now	*now*
☐ Don't disturb me now. **I'm working**.	☐ **I've been working** hard. Now I'm going to have a break.
☐ We need an umbrella. **It's raining**.	☐ The ground is wet. **It's been raining**.
☐ Hurry up! **We're waiting**.	☐ **We've been waiting** for an hour.

Unit 9 - Present perfect continuous (I have been doing)
- exercises

9.1   What have these people been doing or what has been happening?

1	*earlier* *now*

They _'ve been shopping_

2	*earlier* *now*

She _____

3	*earlier* *now*

They _____

4	*earlier* *now*

He _____

9.2   Write a question for each situation.

1   You meet Paul as he is leaving the swimming pool.
   You ask: (you / swim?)   _Have you been swimming?_
2   You have just arrived to meet a friend who is waiting for you.
   You ask: (you / wait / long?) _____
3   You meet a friend in the street. His face and hands are very dirty.
   You ask: (what / you / do?) _____
4   A friend of yours is now working in a shop. You want to know how long.
   You ask: (how long / you / work / there?) _____
5   A friend tells you about his job – he sells computers. You want to know how long.
   You ask: (how long / you / sell / computers?) _____

9.3   Read the situations and complete the sentences.

1   It's raining. The rain started two hours ago.
   It _'s been raining_ for two hours.
2   We are waiting for the bus. We started waiting 20 minutes ago.
   We _____ for 20 minutes.
3   I'm learning Spanish. I started classes in December.
   I _____ since December.
4   Mary is working in London. She started working there on 18 January.
   _____ since 18 January.
5   Our friends always spend their holidays in Italy. They started going there years ago.
   _____ for years.

9.4   Put the verb into the present continuous (**I am –ing**) or present perfect continuous
(**I have been –ing**).

1   _Maria has been learning_ (Maria / learn) English for two years.
2   Hello, Tom. _____ (I / look) for you. Where have you been?
3   Why _____ (you / look) at me like that? Stop it!
4   Linda is a teacher. _____ (she / teach) for ten years.
5   _____ (I / think) about what you said and I've decided to take your
   advice.
6   'Is Paul on holiday this week?'   'No, _____ (he / work).'
7   Sarah is very tired. _____ (she / work) very hard recently.

1

Unit 10 - Present perfect continuous and simple - lesson

Study this example situation:

Kate's clothes are covered in paint.
She **has been painting** the ceiling.

Has been painting is the *present perfect continuous.*

We are interested in the activity. It does not matter whether something has been finished or not. In this example, the activity (painting the ceiling) has not been finished.

The ceiling was white. Now it is red.
She **has painted** the ceiling.

Has painted is the *present perfect simple.*

Here, the important thing is that something has been finished. **Has painted** is a completed action. We are interested in the result of the activity (the painted ceiling), not the activity itself.

Compare these examples:

- □ My hands are very dirty. **I've been repairing** the car.
- □ Joe **has been eating** too much recently. He should eat less.
- □ It's nice to see you again. What **have you been doing** since we last met?
- □ Where have you been? **Have you been playing** tennis?

- □ The car is OK again now. I've **repaired** it.
- □ Somebody **has eaten** all my chocolates. The box is empty.
- □ Where's the book I gave you? What **have** you **done** with it?
- □ **Have you ever played** tennis?

We use the continuous to say *how long* (for an activity that is still happening):

- □ How long **have** you **been reading** that book?
- □ Lisa is still writing letters. She's **been writing** letters **all day.**
- □ They've **been playing** tennis since 2 o'clock.
- □ I'm learning Spanish, but I **haven't been learning** it very long.

We use the simple to say *how much, how many* or *how many times* (for completed actions):

- □ How much of that book **have you read**?
- □ Lisa **has written** ten letters today.
- □ They've **played** tennis three times this week.
- □ I'm learning Spanish, but I **haven't learnt** very much yet.

Some verbs (for example, **know/like/believe**) are not normally used in the continuous:
- □ **I've known** about it for a long time. (*not* I've been knowing)

For a list of these verbs, see Unit 4A. But note that you *can* use **want** and **mean** in the present perfect continuous:
- □ **I've been meaning** to phone Jane, but I keep forgetting.

Unit 10 - Present perfect continuous and simple - exercises

10.1 For each situation, write two sentences using the words in brackets.

1 Tom started reading a book two hours ago. He is still reading it and now he is on page 53.
(read / for two hours) _He has been reading for two hours._
(read / 53 pages so far) _He has read 53 pages so far._

2 Rachel is from Australia. She is travelling round Europe at the moment. She began her trip three months ago.
(travel / for three months) She ....
(visit / six countries so far) ....

3 Patrick is a tennis player. He began playing tennis when he was ten years old. This year he is national champion again – for the fourth time.
(win / the national championships / four times) ....
(play / tennis since he was ten) ....

4 When they left college, Lisa and Sue started making films together. They still make films.
(make / five films since they left college) They ....
(make / films since they left college) ....

10.2 For each situation, ask a question using the words in brackets.

1 You have a friend who is learning Arabic. You ask:
(how long / learn / Arabic?) _How long have you been learning Arabic?_

2 You have just arrived to meet a friend. She is waiting for you. You ask:
(wait / long?) Have ....

3 You see somebody fishing by the river. You ask:
(catch / any fish?) ....

4 Some friends of yours are having a party next week. You ask:
(how many people / invite?) ....

5 A friend of yours is a teacher. You ask:
(how long / teach?) ....

6 You meet somebody who is a writer. You ask:
(how many books / write?) ....
(how long / write / books?) ....

7 A friend of yours is saving money to go on holiday. You ask:
(how long / save?) ....
(how much money / save?) ....

10.3 Put the verb into the more suitable form, present perfect simple (I have done) or continuous (I have been doing).

1 Where have you been? _Have you been playing_ (you / play) tennis?

2 Look! .... (somebody / break) that window.

3 You look tired. .... (you / work) hard?

4 '.. (you / ever / work) in a factory?' 'No, never.'

5 'Liz is away on holiday.' 'Is she? Where .... (she / go)?

6 My brother is an actor. .... (he / appear) in several films.

7 'Sorry I'm late.' 'That's all right. .... (I / not / wait) long.'

8 'Is it still raining?' 'No, ... (it / stop).'

9 .... (I / lose) my address book. .... (you / see) it?

10 .... (I / read) the book you lent me, but .... (I / not / finish) it yet. It's very interesting.

11 .... (I / read) the book you lent me, so you can have it back now.

Unit 11 - How long have you (been)… ? - lesson

Study this example situation:

Dan and Jenny are married. They got married exactly 20 years ago, so today is their 20th wedding anniversary.

They **have been** married **for 20 years.**

We say: They **are** married. *(present)*

but   **How long have they been** married? *(present perfect)*
           (*not* How long are they married?)
           They **have been** married **for 20 years.**
           (*not* They are married for 20 years)

We use the *present perfect* to talk about something that began in the past and still continues now. Compare the *present* and the *present perfect*:

☐ Bill **is** in hospital.
but He **has been** in hospital **since Monday.**
        (*not* Bill is in hospital since Monday)

☐ **Do** you **know** each other well?
but **Have** you **known** each other **for a long time?**
        (*not* Do you know)

☐ She's **waiting** for somebody.
but She's **been waiting all morning.**

☐ **Do** they **have** a car?
but **How long have** they **had** their car?

present

present perfect

now

I have known/had/lived etc. is the *present perfect simple.*
I have been learning / been waiting / been doing etc. is the *present perfect continuous.*

When we ask or say 'how long', the continuous is more usual (see Unit 10):
☐ I've **been learning** English **for six months.**
☐ It's **been raining since lunchtime.**
☐ Richard **has been doing** the same job **for 20 years.**
☐ '**How long have** you **been driving?**' 'Since I was 17.'

Some verbs (for example, **know/like/believe**) are not normally used in the continuous:
☐ How long **have** you **known** Jane? (*not* have you been knowing)
☐ I've **had** a pain in my stomach all day. (*not* I've been having)
See also Units 4A and 10C. For **have**, see Unit 17.

You can use either the present perfect continuous or simple with **live** and **work:**
☐ Julia **has been living / has lived** in Paris for a long time.
☐ How long **have** you **been working / have** you **worked** here?

But we use the simple (**I've lived / I've done** etc.) with **always:**
☐ I've **always lived** in the country. (*not* always been living)

We say 'I **haven't done** something **since/for** …' (*present perfect simple*):
☐ I **haven't seen** Tom since Monday. (= Monday was the last time I saw him)
☐ Sue **hasn't phoned** for ages. (= the last time she phoned was ages ago)

Unit 11 - How long have you (been)... ? - exercises

11.1 Are the <u>underlined</u> verbs right or wrong? Correct them where necessary.
1 Bob is a friend of mine. <u>I know him</u> very well. — OK
2 Bob is a friend of mine. <u>I know him</u> for a long time. — I've known him
3 Sue and Alan <u>are married</u> since July.
4 The weather is awful. <u>It's raining</u> again.
5 The weather is awful. <u>It's raining</u> all day.
6 I like your house. How long <u>are you living</u> there?
7 Gary <u>is working</u> in a shop for the last few months.
8 <u>I don't know</u> Tim well. We've only met a few times.
9 I gave up drinking coffee. I <u>don't drink</u> it for a year.
10 That's a very old bike. How long <u>do you have</u> it?

11.2 Read the situations and write questions from the words in brackets.
1 John tells you that his mother is in hospital. You ask him:
(how long / be / in hospital?) — How long has your mother been in hospital?
2 You meet a woman who tells you that she teaches English. You ask her:
(how long / teach / English?)
3 You know that Jane is a good friend of Caroline's. You ask Jane:
(how long / know / Caroline?)
4 Your friend's brother went to Australia some time ago and he's still there. You ask your friend:
(how long / be / in Australia?)
5 Tim always wears the same jacket. It's a very old jacket. You ask him:
(how long / have / that jacket?)
6 You are talking to a friend about Joe. Joe now works at the airport. You ask your friend:
(how long / work / at the airport?)
7 A friend of yours is learning to drive. You ask him:
(how long / learn / to drive?)
8 You meet somebody on a plane. She says that she lives in Chicago. You ask her:
(always / live / in Chicago?)

11.3 Complete B's answers to A's questions.

	A	B
1	Bill is in hospital, isn't he?	Yes, he __has been__ in hospital since Monday.
2	Do you see Ann very often?	No, I __haven't seen__ her for three months.
3	Is Margaret married?	Yes, she ____ married for ten years.
4	Are you waiting for me?	Yes, I ____ for the last half hour.
5	You know Linda, don't you?	Yes, we ____ each other a long time.
6	Do you still play tennis?	No, I ____ tennis for years.
7	Is Jim watching TV?	Yes, he ____ TV all evening.
8	Do you watch TV a lot?	No, I ____ TV for ages.
9	Have you got a headache?	Yes, I ____ a headache all morning.
10	George is never ill, is he?	No, he ____ ill since I've known him.
11	Are you feeling ill?	Yes, I ____ ill all day.
12	Sue lives in London, doesn't she?	Yes, she ____ in London for the last few years.
13	Do you go to the cinema a lot?	No, I ____ to the cinema for ages.
14	Would you like to go to New York one day?	Yes, I ____ to go to New York. (*use* **always / want**)

27

Unit 12 - For and since/When… ? and how long… ? - lesson

We use **for** and **since** to say how long something has been happening.

We use **for** + a period of time (**two hours, six weeks** etc.):

□ I've been waiting **for two hours**.

for two hours
two hours ago ──────► *now*

for		
two hours	a long time	a week
20 minutes	six months	ages
five days	50 years	years

□ Sally has been working here **for six months**. (*not* since six months)
□ I haven't seen Tom **for three days**. (*not* since three days)

We use **since** + the start of a period (**8 o'clock, Monday, 1999** etc.):

□ I've been waiting **since 8 o'clock**.

since 8 o'clock
8 o'clock ──────► *now*

since		
8 o'clock	April	lunchtime
Monday	1985	we arrived
12 May	Christmas	I got up

□ Sally has been working here **since April**. (= from April until now)
□ I haven't seen Tom **since Monday**. (= from Monday until now)

It is possible to leave out **for** (but not usually in negative sentences):

□ They've been married (for) **ten years**. (with or without **for**)
□ They **haven't had** a holiday **for** ten years. (you must use **for**)

We do *not* use **for** + all … (**all day** / **all my life** etc.):

□ I've lived here **all my life**. (*not* for all my life)

Compare **when** … ? (+ *past simple*) and **how long** … ? (+ *present perfect*):

A: **When** did it start raining?
B: It started raining **an hour ago** / **at 1 o'clock**.

A: **How long** has it been raining?
B: It's been raining **for an hour** / **since 1 o'clock**.

A: **When** did Joe and Carol first meet?
B: They first met { **a long time ago.** / **when they were at school.** }

A: **How long** have they known each other?
B: They've known each other { **for a long time.** / **since they were at school.** }

We say 'It's (a long time / two years etc.) **since** something happened':

□ It's **two years since** I last saw Joe. (= I **haven't seen** Joe for two years)
□ It's **ages since** we went to the cinema. (= We **haven't been** to the cinema for ages)

You can ask 'How long is it **since** … ?':

□ **How long is it since** you last saw Joe? (= When did you last see Joe?)
□ **How long is it since** Mrs Hill died? (= When did Mrs Hill die?)

You can also say 'It's been (= It has been) … **since** … ':

□ It's **been** two years since I last saw Joe.

28

Unit 12 - For and since/When... ? and how long... ? - exercises

12.1 Write **for** or **since**.
1 It's been raining ..... *since* ..... lunchtime.
2 Sarah has lived in Paris .... 1995.
3 Paul has lived in London .... ten years.
4 I'm tired of waiting. We've been sitting here .... an hour.
5 Kevin has been looking for a job .... he left school.
6 I haven't been to a party .... ages.
7 I wonder where Joe is. I haven't seen him .... last week.
8 Jane is away. She's been away .... Friday.
9 The weather is dry. It hasn't rained .... a few weeks.

12.2 Write questions with **how long** and **when**.
1 It's raining.
   (how long?) ..... *How long has it been raining?* .....
   (when?) ..... *When did it start raining?* .....
2 Kate is learning Japanese.
   (how long / learn?) ....
   (when / start?) ....
3 I know Simon.
   (how long / you / know?) ....
   (when / you / first / meet?) ....
4 Rebecca and David are married.
   (how long?) ....
   (when?) ....

12.3 Read the situations and complete the sentences.
1 It's raining. It's been raining since lunchtime. It ..... *started raining* ..... at lunchtime.
2 Ann and Sue are friends. They first met years ago. They've ..... *known each other for* ..... years.
3 Joe is ill. He became ill on Sunday. He has .... Sunday.
4 Joe is ill. He became ill a few days ago. He has .... a few days.
5 Liz is married. She's been married for a year. She got ....
6 You have a headache. It started when you woke up.
   I've .... I woke up.
7 Sue has been in Italy for the last three weeks.
   She went ....
8 You're working in a hotel. You started six months ago.
   I've ....

12.4 Write B's sentences using the words in brackets.
1 A: Do you often go on holiday?
   B: (no / five years) ..... *No, I haven't had a holiday for five years* .....
2 A: Do you often see Sarah?
   B: (no / about a month) No, ...
3 A: Do you often go to the cinema?
   B: (no / a long time) ....
4 A: Do you often eat in restaurants?
   B: (no / ages) No, I ....

Now write B's answers again. This time use It's ... since ... .
5 (1) ..... *No, it's five years since I had a holiday.* .....
6 (2) No, ...
7 (3) ....
8 (4) No, it's ....

2

Unit 13 - Present perfect and past 1 - lesson

Study this example situation:

Tom is looking for his key. He can't find it.

He **has lost** his key. (*present perfect*)

This means that he doesn't have his key *now*.

Ten minutes later:

Now Tom **has found** his key. He has it now.

Has he **lost** his key?   No, he **has found** it.

Did he **lose** his key?   Yes, he **did**.

He **lost** his key   (*past simple*)

but now he **has found** it.   (*present perfect*)

The present perfect (something **has happened**) is a *present* tense. It always tells us about the situation *now*. 'Tom **has lost** his key' = he doesn't have his key *now* (see Unit 7).

The past simple (something **happened**) tells us only about the *past*. If somebody says 'Tom **lost** his key', this doesn't tell us whether he has the key now or not. It tells us only that he lost his key at some time in the past.

Do *not* use the present perfect if the situation now is different. Compare:
- ☐ They've **gone** away. They'll be back on Friday. (they are away *now*)
  They **went** away, but I think they're back at home now. (*not* They've gone)

- ☐ It **has stopped** raining now, so we don't need the umbrella. (it isn't raining *now*)
  It **stopped** raining for a while, but now it's raining again. (*not* It has stopped)

You can use the present perfect for new or recent happenings:
- ☐ 'I've **repaired** the TV. It's working OK now.' 'Oh, that's good.'
- ☐ Have you heard the news? Sally **has won** the lottery!

Use the past simple (*not* the present perfect) for things that are not recent or new:
- ☐ Mozart **was** a composer. He **wrote** more than 600 pieces of music.
  (*not* has been ... has written)
- ☐ My mother **grew** up in Scotland. (*not* has grown)

Compare:
- ☐ Did you know that somebody **has invented** a new type of washing machine?
- ☐ Who **invented** the telephone? (*not* has invented)

We use the present perfect to give new information (see Unit 7). But if we continue to talk about it, we normally use the past simple:
- ☐ A: Ow! I've **burnt** myself.
  B: How **did** you **do** that? (*not* have you done)
  A: I **picked** up a hot dish. (*not* have picked)
- ☐ A: Look! Somebody **has spilt** something on the sofa.
  B: Well, it **wasn't** me. I **didn't** do it. (*not* hasn't been ... haven't done)

Unit 13 - Present perfect and past 1 - exercises

13.1 Complete the sentences using the verbs in brackets. Use the present perfect where possible. Otherwise use the past simple.

1	2
I can't get in. I _'ve lost_ (lose) my key.	The office is empty now. Everybody .... (go) home.
3	4
I meant to call you last night, but I .... (forget).	Mary .... (go) to Egypt for a holiday, but she's back home in England now. MARY
5	6
Are you OK? Yes, I .... (have) a headache, but I feel fine now.	Can you help us? Our car .... (break) down.

13.2 Put the verb into the correct form, present perfect or past simple.

1 It _stopped_ raining for a while, but now it's raining again. (stop)
2 The town is very different now. It _has changed_ a lot. (change)
3 I did German at school, but I .... most of it now. (forget)
4 The police .... three people, but later they let them go. (arrest)
5 What do you think of my English? Do you think it .... ? (improve)
6 A: Are you still reading the paper?
   B: No, I .... with it. You can have it. (finish)
7 I .... for a job as a tourist guide, but I wasn't successful. (apply)
8 Where's my bike? It .... outside the house, but it's not there now. (be)
9 Look! There's an ambulance over there. There .... an accident. (be)
10 A: Have you heard about Ben? He .... his arm. (break)
    B: Really? How .... that .... ? (happen)
    A: He .... off a ladder. (fall)

13.3 Are the underlined parts of these sentences right or wrong? Correct them where necessary.

1 Do you know about Sue? She's given up her job.   OK
2 My mother has grown up in Scotland.   grew
3 How many plays has Shakespeare written? ....
4 Ow! I've cut my finger. It's bleeding. ....
5 Drugs have become a big problem everywhere. ....
6 The Chinese have invented paper. ....
7 Where have you been born? ....
8 Mary isn't at home. She's gone shopping. ....
9 Albert Einstein has been the scientist who has developed the theory of relativity. ....

27

Unit 14 - Present perfect and past 2 - lesson

Do not use the present perfect (**I have done**) when you talk about a *finished* time (for example, **yesterday / ten minutes ago / in 1999 / when I was a child**). Use a past tense:

☐ It **was** very cold **yesterday**. (*not* has been)

☐ Paul and Lucy **arrived ten minutes ago**. (*not* have arrived)

☐ **Did** you **eat** a lot of sweets **when you were a child**? (*not* have you eaten)

☐ I **got** home late **last night**. I **was** very tired and **went** straight to bed.

Use the past to ask **When ... ?** or **What time ... ?**:

☐ **When did** your friends **arrive**? (*not* have ... arrived)

☐ **What time did** you **finish** work?

Compare:

Present perfect	*Past simple*
☐ Tom **has lost** his key. He can't get into the house.	☐ Tom **lost** his key **yesterday**. He couldn't get into the house.
☐ Is Carla here or **has** she **left**?	☐ **When did** Carla **leave**?

Compare:

Present perfect (**have done**)	*Past simple* (**did**)
☐ I've **done** a lot of work **today**.	☐ I **did** a lot of work **yesterday**.
We use the present perfect for a period of time that continues *until now*. For example: **today / this week / since 1985**.	We use the past simple for a *finished* time in the past. For example: **yesterday / last week / from 1995 to 2001**.

┌─*unfinished*─┐	┌─*finished*─┐
today	**yesterday**
past *now*	*past* *now*

☐ It **hasn't rained this week**.	☐ It **didn't rain last week**.
☐ **Have** you **seen** Anna **this morning**? (it is still morning)	☐ **Did** you **see** Anna **this morning**? (it is now afternoon or evening)
☐ **Have** you **seen** Tim **recently**?	☐ **Did** you **see** Tim **on Sunday**?
☐ I don't know where Lisa is. I **haven't seen** her. (= I haven't seen her recently)	☐ A: **Was** Lisa at the party **on Sunday**? B: I don't think so. I **didn't see** her.
☐ We've **been waiting** for an hour. (we are still waiting now)	☐ We **waited** (*or* **were waiting**) for an hour. (we are no longer waiting)
☐ Ian lives in London. He **has lived** there for seven years.	☐ Ian **lived** in Scotland for ten years. Now he lives in London.
☐ I **have never played** golf. (in my life)	☐ I **didn't play** golf last summer.
☐ *It's the last day of your holiday. You say:* It's **been** a really good holiday. I've really **enjoyed** it.	☐ *After you come back from holiday you say:* It **was** a really good holiday. I really **enjoyed** it.

Unit 14 - Present perfect and past 2 - exercises

14.1 Are the <u>underlined</u> parts of these sentences right or wrong? Correct them where necessary.

1 <u>I've lost</u> my key. I can't find it anywhere.   OK
2 <u>Have you eaten</u> a lot of sweets when you were a child?   Did you eat
3 <u>I've bought</u> a new car. You must come and see it.   ....
4 <u>I've bought</u> a new car last week.   ....
5 Where <u>have you been</u> yesterday evening?   ....
6 Lucy <u>has left</u> school in 1999.   ....
7 I'm looking for Mike. <u>Have you seen</u> him?   ....
8 '<u>Have you been</u> to Paris?'   'Yes, many times.'   ....
9 I'm very hungry. <u>I haven't eaten</u> much today.   ....
10 When <u>has this book been</u> published?   ....

14.2 Make sentences from the words in brackets. Use the present perfect or past simple.

1 (it / not / rain / this week)   It hasn't rained this week.
2 (the weather / be / cold / recently) The weather ....
3 (it / cold / last week) It ....
4 (I / not / read / a newspaper yesterday) I ....
5 (I / not / read / a newspaper today) ....
6 (Emily / earn / a lot of money / this year) ....
7 (she / not / earn / so much / last year) ....
8 (you / have / a holiday recently?) ....

14.3 Put the verb into the correct form, present perfect or past simple.

1 I don't know where Lisa is.   Have you seen (you / see) her?
2 When I .... (get) home last night, I .... (be) very tired and I .... (go) straight to bed.
3 A: .... (you / finish) painting the bedroom?
   B: Not yet. I'll finish it tomorrow.
4 George .... (not / be) very well last week.
5 Mr Clark .... (work) in a bank for 15 years. Then he gave it up.
6 Molly lives in Dublin. She .... (live) there all her life.
7 A: .... (you / go) to the cinema last night?
   B: Yes, but it .... (be) a mistake. The film .... (be) awful.
8 My grandfather .... (die) before I was born. I .... (never / meet) him.
9 I don't know Carol's husband. I .... (never / meet) him.
10 A: Is Martin here? B: No, he .... (go) out.
    A: When exactly .... (he / go) out? B: About ten minutes ago.
11 A: Where do you live? B: In Boston.
    A: How long .... (you / live) there? B: Five years.
    A: Where .... (you / live) before that? B: In Chicago.
    A: And how long .... (you / live) in Chicago? B: Two years.

14.4 Write sentences about yourself using the ideas in brackets.

1 (something you haven't done today)   I haven't eaten any fruit today.
2 (something you haven't done today) ....
3 (something you didn't do yesterday) ....
4 (something you did yesterday evening) ....
5 (something you haven't done recently) ....
6 (something you've done a lot recently) ....

Unit 15 - Past perfect (I had done) - lesson

Study this example situation:

at 10.30   *at 11.00*

PAUL   SARAH

Sarah went to a party last week. Paul went to the party too, but they didn't see each other. Paul left the party at 10.30 and Sarah arrived at 11 o'clock. So:

When Sarah arrived at the party, Paul wasn't there.

He **had gone** home.

Had gone is the *past perfect (simple)*:

I/we/they/you he/she/it	had	(= I'd etc.) (= he'd etc.)	gone seen finished etc.

The past perfect simple is **had** + *past participle* (**gone/seen/finished** etc).

Sometimes we talk about something that happened in the past:
- □ Sarah **arrived** at the party.

This is the starting point of the story. Then, if we want to talk about things that happened *before* this time, we use the past perfect (**had** ...):
- □ When Sarah arrived at the party, Paul **had** already **gone** home.

Some more examples:
- □ When we got home last night, we found that somebody **had broken** into the flat.
- □ Karen didn't want to go to the cinema with us because she**'d** already **seen** the film.
- □ At first I thought I**'d done** the right thing, but I soon realised that I**'d made** a big mistake.
- □ The man sitting next to me on the plane was very nervous. He **hadn't flown** before.
  or ... He **had** never **flown** before.

Compare the *present perfect* (**have seen** etc.) and the *past perfect* (**had seen** etc.):

Present perfect	Past perfect
have seen	**had seen**
past *now*	*past* *now*
□ Who is that woman? I've never **seen** her before.	□ I didn't know who she was. I'd never **seen** her before. (= before that time)
□ We aren't hungry. We've just **had** lunch.	□ We weren't hungry. We'd just **had** lunch.
□ The house is dirty. They **haven't cleaned** it for weeks.	□ The house was dirty. They **hadn't cleaned** it for weeks.

Compare the *past simple* (**left, was** etc.) and the *past perfect* (**had left, had been** etc.):

- □ A: Was Tom there when you arrived?
  B: Yes, but he **left** soon afterwards.
- □ Kate **wasn't** at home when I phoned. She **was** at her mother's house.

- □ A: Was Tom there when you arrived?
  B: No, he **had** already **left**.
- □ Kate **had** just **got** home when I phoned. She **had been** at her mother's house.

Unit 15 - Past perfect (I had done) - exercises

15.1 Read the situations and write sentences from the words in brackets.
  1 You went to Sue's house, but she wasn't there.
    (she / go / out) __She had gone out.__
  2 You went back to your home town after many years. It wasn't the same as before.
    (it / change / a lot) ....
  3 I invited Rachel to the party, but she couldn't come.
    (she / arrange / to do something else) ....
  4 You went to the cinema last night. You got to the cinema late.
    (the film / already / begin) ....
  5 It was nice to see Dan again after such a long time.
    (I / not / see / him for five years) ....
  6 I offered Sue something to eat, but she wasn't hungry.
    (she / just / have / breakfast) ....

15.2 For each situation, write a sentence ending with **never ... before**. Use the verb in brackets.
  1 The man sitting next to you on the plane was very nervous. It was his first flight.
    (fly) __He'd never flown before.__
  2 A woman walked into the room. She was a complete stranger to me.
    (see) I .... before.
  3 Sam played tennis yesterday. He wasn't very good at it because it was his first game.
    (play) He ....
  4 Last year we went to Denmark. It was our first time there.
    (be there) We ....

15.3 Use the sentences on the left to complete the paragraphs on the right. These sentences are in the order in which they happened – so (1) happened before (2), (2) before (3) etc. But your paragraph begins with the underlined sentence, so sometimes you need the past perfect.

  1 (1) Somebody broke into the office during the night.
    (2) We arrived at work in the morning.
    (3) We called the police.

    We arrived at work in the morning and found that somebody __had broken__ into the office during the night. So we ....

  2 (1) Laura went out this morning.
    (2) I tried to phone her.
    (3) There was no answer.

    I tried to phone Laura this morning, but .... no answer. She .... out.

  3 (1) Jim came back from holiday a few days ago.
    (2) I met him the same day.
    (3) He looked very well.

    I met Jim a few days ago. .... just .... holiday. .... very well.

  4 (1) Kevin sent Sally lots of emails.
    (2) She never replied to them.
    (3) Yesterday he got a phone call from her.
    (4) He was very surprised.

    Yesterday Kevin .... from Sally. He .... very surprised. He .... lots of emails, but she ....

15.4 Put the verb into the correct form, past perfect (**I had done**) or past simple (**I did**).
  1 'Was Paul at the party when you arrived?' 'No, he __had gone__ (go) home.'
  2 I felt very tired when I got home, so I .... (go) straight to bed.
  3 The house was very quiet when I got home. Everybody .... (go) to bed.
  4 Sorry I'm late. The car .... (break) down on my way here.
  5 We were driving along the road when we .... (see) a car which .... (break) down, so we .... (stop) to help.

Unit 16 - Past perfect continuous (I had been doing) - lesson

Study this example situation:

yesterday morning

Yesterday morning I got up and looked out of the window. The sun was shining, but the ground was very wet.

It **had been** raining.

It was *not* raining when I looked out of the window; the sun was shining. But it **had been** raining before.

Had been -ing is the *past perfect continuous*:

I/we/you/they he/she/it	had	(= I'd etc.) (= he'd etc.)	been	doing working playing etc.

Some more examples:

- □ When the boys came into the house, their clothes were dirty, their hair was untidy and one of them had a black eye. They'**d been fighting**.
- □ I was very tired when I got home. I'**d been working** hard all day.
- □ When I went to Madrid a few years ago, I stayed with a friend of mine. She'**d been living** there only a short time but knew the city very well.

You can say that something **had been happening** for a period of time before something else happened:

- □ We'**d been playing** tennis for about half an hour when it started to rain heavily.
- □ George went to the doctor last Friday. He **hadn't been feeling** well for some time.

Compare **have been -ing** (*present perfect continuous*) and **had been -ing** (*past perfect continuous*):

Present perfect continuous	*Past perfect continuous*
I have been -ing	**I had been -ing**
past *now*	*past* *now*

- □ I hope the bus comes soon. I'**ve been waiting** for 20 minutes. *(before now)*
- □ James is out of breath. He **has been running**.

- □ At last the bus came. I'**d been waiting** for 20 minutes. *(before the bus came)*
- □ James was out of breath. He **had been running**.

Compare **was -ing** (*past continuous*) and **had been -ing**:

- □ It **wasn't raining** when we went out. The sun **was shining**. But it **had been raining**, so the ground was wet.
- □ Cathy **was sitting** in an armchair resting. She was tired because she'**d been working** very hard.

Some verbs (for example, **know** and **like**) are not normally used in the continuous:

- □ We were good friends. We **had known** each other for years. (*not* had been knowing)

For a list of these verbs, see Unit 4A.

Unit 16 - Past perfect continuous (I had been doing) - exercises

16.1 Read the situations and make sentences from the words in brackets.

1 I was very tired when I arrived home.
(I / work / hard all day) _I'd been working hard all day._
2 The two boys came into the house. They had a football and they were both very tired.
(they / play / football) ....
3 I was disappointed when I had to cancel my holiday.
(I / look / forward to it) ....
4 Ann woke up in the middle of the night. She was frightened and didn't know where she was.
(she / dream) ....
5 When I got home, Tom was sitting in front of the TV. He had just turned it off.
(he / watch / a film) ....

16.2 Read the situations and complete the sentences.

1 We played tennis yesterday. Half an hour after we began playing, it started to rain.
We _had been playing for half an hour_ when _it started to rain_ .

2 I had arranged to meet Tom in a restaurant. I arrived and waited for him. After 20 minutes
I suddenly realised that I was in the wrong restaurant.
I .... for 20 minutes when I ....
.... the wrong restaurant.

3 Sarah got a job in factory. Five years later the factory closed down.
At the time the factory .... , Sarah ....
.... there for five years.

4 I went to a concert last week. The orchestra began playing. After about ten minutes a man in
the audience suddenly started shouting.
The orchestra .... when
....

This time make your own sentence:

5 I began walking along the road. I ....
when ....

16.3 Put the verb into the most suitable form, past continuous (**I was doing**), past perfect
(**I had done**) or past perfect continuous (**I had been doing**).

1 It was very noisy next door. Our neighbours _were having_ (have) a party.
2 We were good friends. We _had known_ (know) each other for years.
3 John and I went for a walk. I had difficulty keeping up with him because he
.... (walk) so fast.
4 Sue was sitting on the ground. She was out of breath. She .... (run).
5 When I arrived, everybody was sitting round the table with their mouths full. They
.... (eat).
6 When I arrived, everybody was sitting round the table and talking. Their mouths were empty,
but their stomachs were full. They .... (eat).
7 Jim was on his hands and knees on the floor. He .... (look) for his
contact lens.
8 When I arrived, Kate .... (wait) for me. She was annoyed with me
because I was late and she .... (wait) for a long time.
9 I was sad when I sold my car. I .... (have) it for a very long time.
10 We were extremely tired at the end of the journey. We .... (travel) for
more than 24 hours.

Unit 17 - Have got and have - lesson

Have got and **have** (= for possession, relationships, illnesses etc.)

You can use **have got** or **have** (without **got**). There is no difference in meaning:
- □ They've **got** a new car.   *or*   They **have** a new car.
- □ Lisa's **got** two brothers.   *or*   Lisa **has** two brothers.
- □ I've **got** a headache.   *or*   I **have** a headache.
- □ Our house **has got** a small garden.   *or*   Our house **has** a small garden.
- □ He's **got** a few problems.   *or*   He **has** a few problems.

With these meanings (possession etc.), you cannot use continuous forms (**am having** etc.):
- □ We're enjoying our holiday. We've **got** / We **have** a nice room in the hotel. (*not* We're having)

For the past we use **had** (without **got**):
- □ Lisa **had** long hair when she was a child. (*not* Lisa had got)

In questions and negative sentences there are three possible forms:

Have you got any questions?	I **haven't got** any questions.
Do you have any questions?	I **don't have** any questions.
Have you any questions? *(less usual)*	I **haven't** any questions. *(less usual)*
Has she got a car?	She **hasn't got** a car.
Does she have a car?	She **doesn't have** a car.
Has she a car? *(less usual)*	She **hasn't** a car. *(less usual)*

In past questions and negative sentences, we use **did/didn't**:
- □ **Did** you **have** a car when you were living in London?
- □ I **didn't have** a watch, so I didn't know the time.
- □ Lisa **had** long hair, **didn't** she?

Have breakfast / have a bath / have a good time etc.

We also use **have** (*but not* have got) for many actions and experiences. For example:

have	breakfast / dinner / a cup of coffee / something to eat etc.
	a bath / a shower / a swim / a break / a rest / a party / a holiday
	an accident / an experience / a dream
	a look (at something)
	a chat / a conversation / a discussion (with somebody)
	difficulty / trouble / fun / a good time etc.
	a baby (= give birth to a baby)

Have got is *not* possible in the expressions in the box. Compare:
- □ Sometimes I **have** (= eat) a sandwich for my lunch. (*not* I've got)
but   I've **got** / I **have** some sandwiches. Would you like one?

You can use continuous forms (**am having** etc.) with the expressions in the box:
- □ We're enjoying our holiday. We're **having** a great time. (*not* We have)
- □ Mike **is having** a shower at the moment. He has a shower every day.

In questions and negative sentences we use **do/does/did**:
- □ I **don't** usually **have** a big breakfast. (*not* I usually haven't)
- □ What time **does** Jenny **have** lunch? (*not* has Jenny lunch)
- □ **Did** you **have** difficulty finding a place to live?

Unit 17 - Have got and have - exercises

17.1 Write negative sentences with **have**. Some are present (**can't**) and some are past (**couldn't**).

1 I can't get into the house. (a key) _I haven't got a key._
2 I couldn't read the letter. (my glasses) _I didn't have my glasses._
3 I can't get onto the roof. (a ladder) I ....
4 We couldn't visit the museum. (enough time) We ....
5 He couldn't find his way to our house. (a map) ....
6 She can't pay her bills. (any money) ....
7 I can't go swimming today. (enough energy) ....
8 They couldn't take any photographs. (a camera) ....

17.2 Complete the questions with **have**. Some are present and some are past.

1 Excuse me, _have you got_ a pen I could borrow?
2 Why are you holding your face like that? .... a toothache?
3 .... a lot of toys when you were a child?
4 A: .... the time, please?
   B: Yes, it's ten past seven.
5 I need a stamp for this letter. .... one?
6 When you worked in your last job, ... your own office?
7 A: It started to rain very heavily while I was out.
   B: .... an umbrella?

17.3 Write sentences about yourself. Have you got these things now? Did you have them ten years ago?
Write two sentences each time using **I've got / I haven't got** and **I had / I didn't have**.
(You can also write about your family: **We've got ... / We had ...** etc.).

now	*ten years ago*
1 (a car) _I've got a car._	_I didn't have a car._
2 (a bike) I	I ....
3 (a mobile phone)	....
4 (a dog)	....
5 (a guitar)	....
6 (long hair)	....
7 (a driving licence)	....

17.4 Complete the sentences. Use an expression from the list and put the verb into the correct form where necessary.

have a baby   have a break   have a chat   have difficulty   have a good flight
have a look   have lunch   have a party   have a nice time   have a shower

1 I don't eat much during the day. I never _have lunch_ .
2 David starts work at 8 o'clock and .... at 10.30.
3 We .... last week. It was great – we invited lots of people.
4 Excuse me, can I .... at your newspaper, please?
5 Jim is away on holiday at the moment. I hope he ....
6 I met Ann in the supermarket yesterday. We stopped and ....
7 A: .... finding the book you wanted?
   B: No, I found it OK.
8 Suzanne .... a few weeks ago. It's her second child.
9 A: Why didn't you answer the phone?
   B: I ....
10 *You meet your friend Sally at the airport. She has just arrived. You say:*
    Hi, Sally. How are you? .... ?

Unit 18 - Used to (do) - lesson

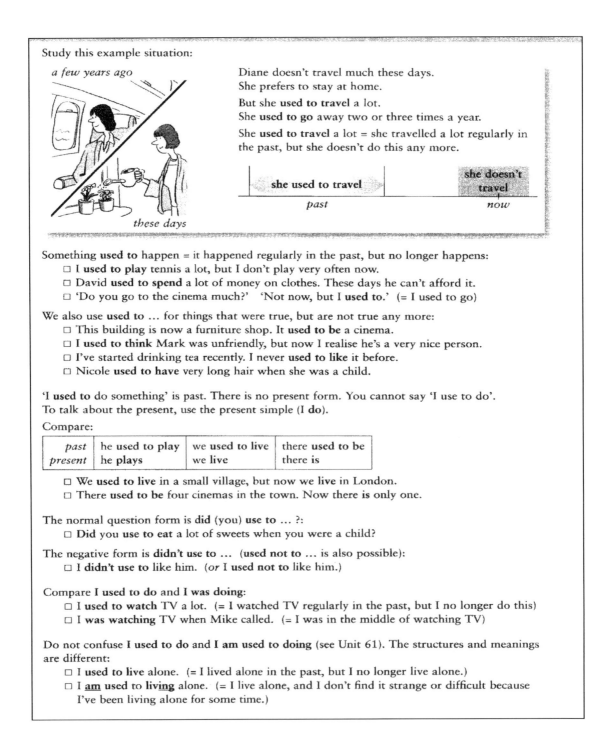

Study this example situation:

a few years ago

Diane doesn't travel much these days.
She prefers to stay at home.

But she **used to travel** a lot.
She **used to go** away two or three times a year.

She **used to travel** a lot = she travelled a lot regularly in the past, but she doesn't do this any more.

she used to travel	she doesn't travel
past	*now*

these days

Something **used to** happen = it happened regularly in the past, but no longer happens:
- □ I **used to play** tennis a lot, but I don't play very often now.
- □ David **used to spend** a lot of money on clothes. These days he can't afford it.
- □ 'Do you go to the cinema much?' 'Not now, but I **used to.**' (= I used to go)

We also use **used to** ... for things that were true, but are not true any more:
- □ This building is now a furniture shop. It **used to be** a cinema.
- □ I **used to think** Mark was unfriendly, but now I realise he's a very nice person.
- □ I've started drinking tea recently. I never **used to like** it before.
- □ Nicole **used to have** very long hair when she was a child.

'I **used to do** something' is past. There is no present form. You cannot say 'I use to do'.
To talk about the present, use the present simple (I **do**).

Compare:

past	he **used to play**	we **used to live**	there **used to be**
present	he **plays**	we live	there **is**

- □ We **used to live** in a small village, but now we live in London.
- □ There **used to be** four cinemas in the town. Now there **is** only one.

The normal question form is **did** (you) **use to** ... ?:
- □ **Did** you **use to eat** a lot of sweets when you were a child?

The negative form is **didn't use to** ... (**used not to** ... is also possible):
- □ I **didn't use to** like him. (*or* I **used not to** like him.)

Compare I **used to do** and I **was doing**:
- □ I **used to watch** TV a lot. (= I watched TV regularly in the past, but I no longer do this)
- □ I **was watching** TV when Mike called. (= I was in the middle of watching TV)

Do not confuse I **used to do** and I **am used to doing** (see Unit 61). The structures and meanings are different:
- □ I **used to live** alone. (= I lived alone in the past, but I no longer live alone.)
- □ I **am** used to **living** alone. (= I live alone, and I don't find it strange or difficult because I've been living alone for some time.)

Unit 18 - Used to (do) - exercises

18.1 Complete the sentences with **use(d) to** + a suitable verb.

1 Diane doesn't travel much now. She ___used to travel___ a lot, but she prefers to stay at home these days.
2 Liz _____ a motorbike, but last year she sold it and bought a car.
3 We came to live in London a few years ago. We _____ in Leeds.
4 I rarely eat ice-cream now, but I _____ it when I was a child.
5 Jim _____ my best friend, but we aren't good friends any longer.
6 It only takes me about 40 minutes to get to work now that the new road is open. It _____ more than an hour.
7 There _____ a hotel near the airport, but it closed a long time ago.
8 When you lived in New York, _____ to the theatre very often?

18.2 Matt changed his life style. He stopped doing some things and started doing other things:

He stopped { studying hard / going to bed early / running three miles every morning }   He started { sleeping late / going out in the evening / spending a lot of money }

Write sentences about Matt with **used to** and **didn't use to**.

1   He used to study hard.
2   He didn't use to sleep late.
3   _____
4   _____
5   _____
6   _____

18.3 Compare what Karen said five years ago and what she says today:

FIVE YEARS AGO
I'm a hotel receptionist.
I travel a lot.
I play the piano.
I've got lots of friends.
I never read newspapers.
I'm very lazy.
I don't drink tea.
I don't like cheese.
I've got a dog.
I go to a lot of parties.

TODAY
My dog died two years ago.
I eat lots of cheese now.
I read a newspaper every day now.
I work very hard these days.
I haven't been to a party for ages.
I don't know many people these days.
I haven't played the piano for years.
I work in a bookshop now.
I don't go away much these days.
Tea's great! I like it now.

Now write sentences about how Karen has changed. Use **used to / didn't use to / never used to** in the first part of your sentence.

1   She used to travel a lot,   but she doesn't go away much these days.
2 She used _____ but _____
3   _____ but _____
4   _____ but _____
5   _____ but _____
6   _____ but _____
7   _____ but _____
8   _____ but _____
9   _____ but _____
10   _____ but _____

Unit 19 - Present tenses for the future - lesson

Present continuous (**I am doing**) with a future meaning

This is Ben's diary for next week.

He **is playing** tennis on Monday afternoon.
He **is going** to the dentist on Tuesday morning.
He **is having** dinner with Kate on Friday.

In all these examples, Ben has already decided and arranged to do these things.

I'm doing something (tomorrow) = I have already decided and arranged to do it:
- A: What **are** you **doing** on Saturday evening? (*not* What do you do)
  B: **I'm going** to the theatre. (*not* I go)
- A: What time **is** Cathy **arriving** tomorrow?
  B: Half past ten. **I'm meeting** her at the station.
- **I'm not working** tomorrow, so we can go out somewhere.
- Ian **isn't playing** football next Saturday. He's hurt his leg.

'**I'm going to** (do)' is also possible in these sentences:
- What **are** you **going to do** on Saturday evening?

But the present continuous is more natural for arrangements. See also Unit 20B.

Do not use **will** to talk about what you have arranged to do:
- What **are** you **doing** this evening? (*not* What will you do)
- Alex **is getting** married next month. (*not* will get)

You can also use the present continuous for an action *just before you begin to do it*. This happens especially with verbs of movement (**go/come/leave** etc.):
- I'm tired. **I'm going** to bed now. Goodnight. (*not* I go to bed now)
- 'Tina, are you ready yet?' 'Yes, **I'm coming**.' (*not* I come)

Present simple (**I do**) with a future meaning

We use the present simple when we talk about timetables, programmes etc. (for public transport, cinemas etc.):
- My train **leaves** at 11.30, so I need to be at the station by 11.15.
- What time **does** the film **begin** this evening?
- It's Wednesday tomorrow. / Tomorrow **is** Wednesday.

You can use the present simple to talk about people if their plans are fixed like a timetable:
- I **start** my new job on Monday.
- What time **do** you **finish** work tomorrow?

But the continuous is more usual for personal arrangements:
- What time **are** you **meeting** Ann tomorrow? (*not* do you meet)

Compare:

Present continuous	*Present simple*
What time **are you arriving**?	What time **does the train arrive**?
I'm going to the cinema this evening.	**The film begins** at 8.15 (this evening).

Unit 19 - Present tenses for the future - exercises

19.1 A friend of yours is planning to go on holiday soon. You ask her about her plans.
Use the words in brackets to make your questions.

1 (where / go?) _Where are you going?_   Scotland.
2 (how long / go for?) .... Ten days.
3 (when / leave?) .... Next Friday.
4 (go / alone?) .... No, with a friend.
5 (travel / by car?) .... No, by train.
6 (where / stay?) .... In a hotel.

19.2 Tom wants you to visit him, but you are very busy. Look at your diary for the next few days and explain to him why you can't come.

TOM: Can you come on Monday evening?
YOU: Sorry, but _I'm playing volleyball_ .... (1)
TOM: What about Tuesday evening then?
YOU: No, not Tuesday. I .... (2)
TOM: And Wednesday evening?
YOU: .... (3)
TOM: Well, are you free on Thursday?
YOU: I'm afraid not. .... (4)

19.3 Have you arranged to do anything at these times? Write sentences about yourself.

1 (this evening) _I'm going out this evening._ or _I'm not doing anything this evening._
2 (tomorrow morning) I ....
3 (tomorrow evening) ....
4 (next Sunday) ....
5 (*choose another day or time*) ....

19.4 Put the verb into the more suitable form, present continuous or present simple.

1 I _'m going_ (go) to the cinema this evening.
2 _Does the film begin_ (the film / begin) at 3.30 or 4.30?
3 We .... (have) a party next Saturday. Would you like to come?
4 The art exhibition .... (finish) on 3 May.
5 I .... (not / go) out this evening. I .... (stay) at home.
6 '........................ (you / do) anything tomorrow morning?' 'No, I'm free. Why?'
7 We .... (go) to a concert tonight. It .... (start) at 7.30.
8 I .... (leave) now. I've come to say goodbye.
9 A: Have you seen Liz recently?
   B: No, but we .... (meet) for lunch next week.
10 *You are on the train to London and you ask another passenger:*
   Excuse me. What time .... (this train / get) to London?
11 *You are talking to Helen:*
   Helen, I .... (go) to the supermarket. .... (you / come) with me?
12 *You and a friend are watching television. You say:*
   I'm bored with this programme. What time .... (it / end)?
13 I .... (not / use) the car this evening, so you can have it.
14 Sue .... (come) to see us tomorrow. She .... (travel) by train and her train .... (arrive) at 10.15.

Unit 20 - (I'm) going to (do) - lesson

I **am going to do** something = I have already decided to do it, I intend to do it:
- □ A: **Are** you **going to watch** the late film on TV tonight?
  B: No, **I'm going to have** an early night.
- □ A: I hear Sarah has won some money. What **is** she **going to do** with it?
  B: She's **going to buy** a new car.
- □ **I'm** just **going to make** a quick phone call. Can you wait for me?
- □ This cheese looks horrible. **I'm not going to eat** it.

I am doing and **I am going to do**

We use **I am doing** (*present continuous*) when we say what we have *arranged* to do – for example, arranged to meet somebody, arranged to go somewhere:
- □ What time **are** you **meeting** Ann this evening?
- □ **I'm leaving** tomorrow. I've got my plane ticket.

I **am going to do** something = I've decided to do it (but perhaps not *arranged* to do it):
- □ 'Your shoes are dirty.' 'Yes, I know. **I'm going to clean** them.' (= I've decided to clean them, but I haven't *arranged* to clean them)
- □ I've decided not to stay here any longer. Tomorrow **I'm going to look** for somewhere else to stay.

Often the difference is very small and either form is possible.

You can also say that 'something **is going to happen**' in the future. For example:

The man can't see the wall in front of him.

He **is going to walk** into the wall.

When we say that 'something **is going to happen**', the situation *now* makes this clear. The man is walking towards the wall now, so we can see that he **is going to walk** into it.

situation now   going to   *future happening*

Some more examples:
- □ Look at those black clouds! It's **going to rain**. (the clouds are there now)
- □ I feel terrible. I think **I'm going to be** sick. (I feel terrible now)
- □ The economic situation is bad now and things **are going to get** worse.

I **was going to** (do something) = I intended to do it, but didn't do it:
- □ We **were going to travel** by train, but then we decided to go by car instead.
- □ Peter **was going to do** the exam, but he changed his mind.
- □ I **was** just **going to cross** the road when somebody shouted 'Stop!'

You can say that 'something **was going to happen**' (but didn't happen):
- □ I thought it **was going to rain**, but it didn't.

Unit 20 - (I'm) going to (do) - exercises

20.1 Write a question with **going to** for each situation.

1 Your friend has won some money. You ask:
(what / do with it?) *What are you going to do with it?*

2 Your friend is going to a party tonight. You ask:
(what / wear?) ....

3 Your friend has just bought a new table. You ask:
(where / put it?) ....

4 Your friend has decided to have a party. You ask:
(who / invite?) ....

20.2 Read the situations and complete the dialogues. Use **going to**.

1 You have decided to tidy your room this morning.
FRIEND: Are you going out this morning?
YOU: No, *I'm going to tidy my room.*

2 You bought a sweater, but it doesn't fit you very well. You have decided to take it back.
FRIEND: That sweater is too big for you.
YOU: I know. ....

3 You have been offered a job, but you have decided not to accept it.
FRIEND: I hear you've been offered a job.
YOU: That's right, but ....

4 You have to phone Sarah. It's morning now, and you have decided to phone her tonight.
FRIEND: Have you phoned Sarah yet?
YOU: No, ...

5 You are in a restaurant. The food is awful and you've decided to complain.
FRIEND: This food is awful, isn't it?
YOU: Yes, it's disgusting. ....

20.3 What is going to happen in these situations? Use the words in brackets.

1 There are a lot of black clouds in the sky.
(rain) *It's going to rain.*

2 It is 8.30. Tom is leaving his house. He has to be at work at 8.45, but the journey takes 30 minutes.
(late) He ....

3 There is a hole in the bottom of the boat. A lot of water is coming in through the hole.
(sink) The boat ....

4 Lucy and Chris are driving. There is very little petrol left in the tank. The nearest petrol station is a long way away.
(run out) They ....

20.4 Complete the sentences with **was/were going to** + the following verbs:

buy   give up   have   phone   play   ~~travel~~

1 We *were going to travel* by train, but then we decided to go by car instead.
2 I .... some new clothes yesterday, but I was very busy and didn't have time to go to the shops.
3 Martin and I .... tennis last week, but he was injured.
4 I .... Jane, but I decided to email her instead.
5 A: When I last saw Tim, he .... his job.
   B: That's right, but in the end he decided to stay where he was.
6 We .... a party last week, but some of our friends couldn't come, so we cancelled it.

Unit 21 - Will/shall 1 - lesson

We use **I'll** (= **I will**) when we decide to do something at the time of speaking:
- ☐ Oh, I've left the door open. **I'll go** and shut it.
- ☐ 'What would you like to drink?'   '**I'll have** an orange juice, please.'
- ☐ 'Did you phone Lucy?'   'Oh no, I forgot. **I'll phone** her now.'

You cannot use the *present simple* (I do / I go etc.) in these sentences:
- ☐ **I'll go** and shut the door. (*not* I go and shut)

We often use **I think I'll ...** and **I don't think I'll ...** :
- ☐ I feel a bit hungry. **I think I'll have** something to eat.
- ☐ **I don't think I'll go** out tonight. I'm too tired.

In spoken English the negative of **will** is usually **won't** (= **will not**):
- ☐ I can see you're busy, so I **won't stay** long.

Do *not* use **will** to talk about what you have already decided or arranged to do (see Units 19–20):
- ☐ **I'm going** on holiday next Saturday. (*not* I'll go)
- ☐ **Are** you **working** tomorrow? (*not* Will you work)

We often use **will** in these situations:

Offering to do something
- ☐ That bag looks heavy. **I'll help** you with it. (*not* I help)

Agreeing to do something
- ☐ A: Can you give Tim this book?
- B: Sure, **I'll give** it to him when I see him this afternoon.

Promising to do something
- ☐ Thanks for lending me the money. **I'll pay** you back on Friday.
- ☐ I **won't tell** anyone what happened. I promise.

Asking somebody to do something (**Will you ... ?**)
- ☐ **Will you** please turn the stereo down? I'm trying to concentrate.

You can use **won't** to say that somebody refuses to do something:
- ☐ I've tried to give her advice, but she **won't listen**.
- ☐ The car **won't start**. (= the car 'refuses' to start)

Shall I ... ?   Shall we ... ?

Shall is used mostly in the questions **shall I ... ? / shall we ... ?**

We use **shall I ... ? / shall we ... ?** to ask somebody's opinion (especially in offers or suggestions):
- ☐ **Shall I** open the window? (= Do you want me to open the window?)
- ☐ I've got no money. What **shall I** do? (= What do you suggest?)
- ☐ '**Shall we** go?' 'Just a minute. I'm not ready yet.'
- ☐ Where **shall we** go this evening?

Compare **shall I ... ?** and **will you ... ?**:
- ☐ **Shall I** shut the door? (= Do you want me to shut it?)
- ☐ **Will you** shut the door? (= I want you to shut it)

Unit 21 - Will/shall 1 - exercises

21.1 Complete the sentences with I'll + a suitable verb.

1 I'm too tired to walk home. I think _I'll take_ a taxi.
2 'It's cold in this room.' 'Is it? _____ on the heating then.'
3 A: We haven't got any milk.
    B: Oh, I forgot to buy some. _____ and get some now.
4 'Shall I do the washing-up?' 'No, it's all right. _____ it later.'
5 'I don't know how to use this computer.' 'OK, _____ you.'
6 'Would you like tea or coffee?' '_____ coffee, please.'
7 'Goodbye! Have a nice holiday.' 'Thanks. _____ you a postcard.'
8 Thanks for letting me borrow your camera. _____ it back to you on Monday, OK?
9 'Are you coming with us?' 'No, I think _____ here.'

21.2 Read the situations and write sentences with I **think I'll ...** or **I don't think I'll ...** .

1 It's a bit cold. The window is open and you decide to close it. You say:
    I think I'll close the window.
2 You are feeling tired and it's getting late. You decide to go to bed. You say:
    I think _____
3 A friend of yours offers you a lift in his car, but you decide to walk. You say:
    Thank you, but _____
4 You arranged to play tennis today. Now you decide that you don't want to play. You say:
    I don't think _____
5 You were going to go swimming. Now you decide that you don't want to go. You say:
    _____

21.3 Which is correct? (If necessary, study Units 19–20 first.)

1 'Did you phone Lucy?' 'Oh no, I forgot. ~~I phone~~ / I'll phone her now.' (I'll phone is correct)
2 I can't meet you tomorrow. I'm playing / ~~I'll play~~ tennis. (I'm playing is correct)
3 I meet / I'll meet you outside the hotel in half an hour, OK? 'Yes, that's fine.'
4 'I need some money.' 'OK, I'm lending / I'll lend you some. How much do you need?'
5 I'm having / I'll have a party next Saturday. I hope you can come.
6 'Remember to get a newspaper when you go out.' 'OK. I don't forget / I won't forget.'
7 What time does your train leave / will your train leave tomorrow?
8 I asked Sue what happened, but she doesn't tell / won't tell me.
9 'Are you doing / Will you do anything tomorrow evening?' 'No, I'm free. Why?'
10 I don't want to go out alone. Do you come / Will you come with me?

21.4 What do you say in these situations? Write sentences with **shall I ... ?** or **shall we ... ?**

1 You and a friend want to do something this evening, but you don't know what.
    You ask your friend. _What shall we do this evening?_
2 You try on a jacket in a shop. You are not sure whether to buy it or not. You ask a friend for advice. _____ it?
3 It's Helen's birthday next week. You want to give her a present, but you don't know what. You ask a friend for advice.
    What _____
4 You and a friend are going on holiday together, but you haven't decided where. You ask him/her. _____
5 You and a friend are going out. You haven't decided whether to go by car or to walk. You ask him/her. _____ or _____
6 Your friend wants you to phone later. You don't know what time to phone. You ask him/her.
    _____

Unit 22 - Will/shall 2 - lesson

We do *not* use **will** to say what somebody has already arranged or decided to do:
  □ Diane **is working** next week. (*not* Diane will work)
  □ **Are** you **going to watch** television this evening? (*not* Will you watch)
For 'is working' and '**Are** you **going to** … ?', see Units 19–20.

But often, when we talk about the future, we are *not* talking about what somebody has decided to do. For example:

Kate is doing an exam next week. Chris and Joe are talking about it.

Do you think Kate will pass the exam?

Yes, she'll pass easily.

CHRIS   *JOE*

She'll pass does *not* mean 'she has decided to pass'. Joe is saying what he knows or thinks will happen. He is *predicting* the future.

When we predict a future happening or situation, we use **will/won't**.

Some more examples:
  □ Jill has been away a long time. When she returns, she'**ll find** a lot of changes here.
  □ 'Where **will** you **be** this time next year?' 'I'**ll be** in Japan.'
  □ That plate is hot. If you touch it, you'**ll burn** yourself.
  □ Tom **won't pass** the exam. He hasn't studied hard enough.
  □ When **will** you **get** your exam results?

We often use **will** ('**ll**) with:

probably	□ I'**ll probably** be home late tonight.
I expect	□ I haven't seen Carol today. **I expect** she'**ll** phone this evening.
(I'm) sure	□ Don't worry about the exam. **I'm sure** you'**ll** pass.
(I) think	□ Do you **think** Sarah **will** like the present we bought her?
(I) don't think	□ **I don't think** the exam **will** be very difficult.
I wonder	□ **I wonder** what **will** happen.

After **I hope**, we generally use the present (**will** is also possible):
  □ I hope Kate **passes** the exam. (*or* I hope Kate **will pass** …)
  □ I hope it **doesn't rain** tomorrow.

Generally we use **will** to talk about the future, but sometimes we use **will** to talk about *now*. For example:
  □ Don't phone Ann now. She'**ll be** busy. (= she'll be busy *now*)

I shall … / we shall …

Normally we use **shall** only with I and **we**. You can say:
  I shall *or* **I will** (**I'll**)   **we shall** *or* **we will** (**we'll**)
  □ **I shall** be late this evening. (*or* **I will** be)
  □ **We shall** probably go to Scotland in the summer. (*or* We **will** probably go)
In spoken English we normally use I'll and we'll:
  □ We'**ll** probably go to Scotland.

The negative of **shall** is **shall not** or **shan't**:
  □ I **shan't** be here tomorrow. (*or* I **won't** be)

Do not use **shall** with **he/she/it/you/they**:
  □ She **will** be very angry. (*not* She shall be)

Unit 22 - Will/shall 2 - exercises

22.1 Which form of the verb is correct (or more natural) in these sentences? The verbs are underlined.

1 Diane isn't free on Saturday. <u>She'll work / She's working</u>. (<u>She's working</u> is correct)
2 <u>I'll go / I'm going</u> to a party tomorrow night. Would you like to come too?
3 I think Jenny <u>will get / is getting</u> the job. She has a lot of experience.
4 I can't meet you this evening. A friend of mine <u>will come / is coming</u> to see me.
5 A: Have you decided where to go for your holidays?
   B: Yes, <u>we'll go / we're going</u> to Italy.
6 There's no need to be afraid of the dog. <u>It won't hurt / It isn't hurting</u> you.

22.2 Complete the sentences with **will ('ll)** + the following verbs:

   be   come   get   like   live   look   meet   ~~pass~~

1 Don't worry about the exam. I'm sure you __'ll pass__ .
2 Why don't you try on this jacket? It .... nice on you.
3 You must meet George sometime. I think you .... him.
4 It's raining. Don't go out. You .... wet.
5 Do you think people .... longer in the future?
6 Goodbye. I expect we .... again before long.
7 I've invited Sue to the party, but I don't think she ....
8 When the new road is finished, my journey to work .... much shorter.

22.3 Put in **will ('ll)** or **won't**.

1 Can you wait for me? I __won't__ be very long.
2 There's no need to take an umbrella with you. It .... rain.
3 If you don't eat anything now, you .... be hungry later.
4 I'm sorry about what happened yesterday. It .... happen again.
5 I've got some incredible news! You .... never believe what happened.
6 Don't ask Amanda for advice. She .... know what to do.

22.4 Where do you think you will be at these times? Write true sentences about yourself. Use:

   I'll be …   or   **I'll probably be …**   or   **I don't know where I'll be**

1 (next Monday evening at 7.45)   _I'll be at home._
       or   _I'll probably be at home._
       or   _I don't know where I'll be._

2 (at 5 o'clock tomorrow morning)
....

3 (at 10.30 tomorrow morning)
....

4 (next Saturday afternoon at 4.15)
....

5 (this time next year)
....

22.5 Write questions using **do you think … will … ?** + the following:

   be back   cost   end   get married   happen   ~~like~~   rain

1 I've bought Rosa this picture.   _Do you think she'll like it_ .... ?
2 The weather doesn't look very good. Do you .... ?
3 The meeting is still going on. When do you .... ?
4 My car needs to be repaired. How much .... ?
5 Sally and David are in love. Do .... ?
6 'I'm going out now.' 'OK. What time .... ?'
7 The future situation is uncertain. What .... ?

Unit 23 - I will and I'm going to - lesson

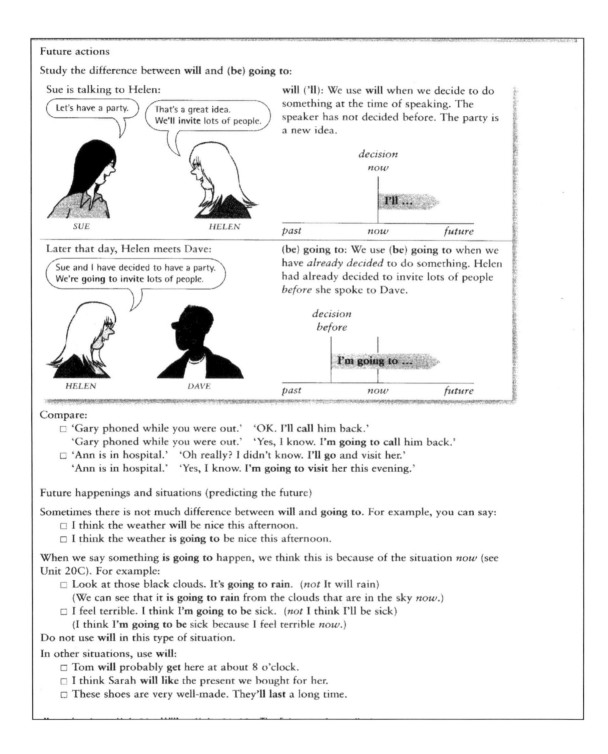

Future actions

Study the difference between **will** and **(be) going to**:

Sue is talking to Helen:

Let's have a party.

That's great idea. We'll invite lots of people.

SUE   HELEN

will ('**ll**): We use **will** when we decide to do something at the time of speaking. The speaker has not decided before. The party is a new idea.

decision now

I'll ...

past   now   future

Later that day, Helen meets Dave:

Sue and I have decided to have a party. We're going to invite lots of people.

HELEN   DAVE

(be) going to: We use **(be) going to** when we have *already decided* to do something. Helen had already decided to invite lots of people *before* she spoke to Dave.

decision before

I'm going to ...

past   now   future

Compare:

☐ 'Gary phoned while you were out.' 'OK. **I'll call** him back.'
'Gary phoned while you were out.' 'Yes, I know. **I'm going to call** him back.'
☐ 'Ann is in hospital.' 'Oh really? I didn't know. **I'll go** and visit her.'
'Ann is in hospital.' 'Yes, I know. **I'm going to visit** her this evening.'

Future happenings and situations (predicting the future)

Sometimes there is not much difference between **will** and **going to**. For example, you can say:

☐ I think the weather **will** be nice this afternoon.
☐ I think the weather **is going to** be nice this afternoon.

When we say something **is going to** happen, we think this is because of the situation *now* (see Unit 20C). For example:

☐ Look at those black clouds. **It's going to rain.** (*not* It will rain)
(We can see that it **is going to rain** from the clouds that are in the sky *now*.)
☐ I feel terrible. I think **I'm going to be sick.** (*not* I think I'll be sick)
(I think **I'm going to be** sick because I feel terrible *now*.)

Do not use **will** in this type of situation.

In other situations, use **will**:

☐ Tom **will** probably **get** here at about 8 o'clock.
☐ I think Sarah **will like** the present we bought for her.
☐ These shoes are very well-made. They'**ll last** a long time.

Unit 23 - I will and I'm going to - exercises

23.1 Complete the sentences using **will** ('ll) or **going to**.

1 A: Why are you turning on the television?
   B: __I'm going to watch__ the news. (I / watch)

2 A: Oh, I've just realised. I haven't got any money.
   B: Haven't you? Well, don't worry. .... you some. (I / lend)

3 A: I've got a headache.
   B: Have you? Wait a second and .... an aspirin for you. (I / get)

4 A: Why are you filling that bucket with water?
   B: .... the car. (I / wash)

5 A: I've decided to repaint this room.
   B: Oh, have you? What colour .... it? (you / paint)

6 A: Where are you going? Are you going shopping?
   B: Yes, ... something for dinner. (I / buy)

7 A: I don't know how to use this camera.
   B: It's easy. .... you. (I / show)

8 A: What would you like to eat?
   B: .... a sandwich, please. (I / have)

9 A: Did you post that letter for me?
   B: Oh, I'm sorry. I completely forgot. .... it now. (I / do)

10 A: The ceiling in this room doesn't look very safe, does it?
    B: No, it looks as if .... down. (it / fall)

11 A: Has George decided what to do when he leaves school?
    B: Yes. Everything is planned. .... a holiday for a few weeks.
    (he / have) Then .... a computer programming course. (he / do)

23.2 Read the situations and complete the sentences using **will** ('ll) or **going to**.

1 The phone rings and you answer. Somebody wants to speak to Jim.
   CALLER: Hello. Can I speak to Jim, please?
   YOU: Just a moment. __I'll get__ him. (I / get)

2 It's a nice day, so you have decided to take a walk. Just before you go, you tell your friend.
   YOU: The weather's too nice to stay in. .... a walk. (I / take)
   FRIEND: Good idea. I think .... you. (I / join)

3 Your friend is worried because she has lost an important letter.
   YOU: Don't worry about the letter. I'm sure .... it. (you / find)
   FRIEND: I hope so.

4 There was a job advertised in the paper recently. At first you were interested, but then you
   decided not to apply.
   FRIEND: Have you decided what to do about that job you were interested in?
   YOU: Yes, ... for it. (I / not / apply)

5 You and a friend come home very late. Other people in the house are asleep. Your friend
   is noisy.
   YOU: Shh! Don't make so much noise. .... everybody up. (you / wake)

6 Paul has to go to the airport to catch a plane tomorrow morning.
   PAUL: Liz, I need somebody to take me to the airport tomorrow morning.
   LIZ: That's no problem. .... you. (I / take) What time is your flight?
   PAUL: 10.50.
   LIZ: OK, ... at about 9 o'clock then. (we / leave)
   Later that day, Joe offers to take Paul to the airport.
   JOE: Paul, do you want me to take you to the airport?
   PAUL: No thanks, Joe. .... me. (Liz / take)

Unit 24 - Will be doing and will have done - lesson

Study this example situation:

These people are standing in a queue to get into the cinema.

now

Half an hour from now, the cinema will be full. Everyone **will be watching** the film.

half an hour from now

Three hours from now, the cinema will be empty. The film **will have finished**. Everybody **will have gone** home.

three hours from now

I **will be doing** something (*future continuous*) = I will be in the middle of doing it:
- ☐ This time next week I'll be on holiday. I'll **be lying** on the beach or **swimming** in the sea.
- ☐ You have no chance of getting the job. You'll **be wasting** your time if you apply for it.

Compare **will be** (do)ing and **will** (do):
- ☐ Don't phone between 7 and 8. We'll **be having** dinner.
- ☐ Let's wait for Liz to arrive and then we'll **have** dinner.

Compare **will be -ing** with other continuous forms:
- ☐ At 10 o'clock yesterday, Sally **was** in her office. She **was working**. *(past)*
  It's 10 o'clock now. She **is** in her office. She **is working**. *(present)*
  At 10 o'clock tomorrow, she **will be** in her office. She **will be working**.

We also use **will be -ing** in a different way: to talk about complete actions in the future.
For example:
- ☐ The government **will be making** a statement about the crisis later today.
- ☐ **Will** you **be going** away this summer?
- ☐ Later in the programme, I'll **be talking** to the Minister of Education ...
- ☐ Our best player is injured and **won't be playing** in the game on Saturday.

Later in the programme I'll be talking to ...

In these examples **will be -ing** is similar to (be) going to ... .

We use **will have** (**done**) (*future perfect*) to say that something will already be complete before a time in the future. For example:
- ☐ Sally always leaves for work at 8.30 in the morning. She won't be at home at 9 o'clock — she'll **have gone** to work.
- ☐ We're late. The film **will** already **have started** by the time we get to the cinema.

Compare **will have** (done) with other perfect forms:
- ☐ Ted and Amy **have been** married for 24 years. *(present perfect)*
  Next year they **will have been** married for 25 years.
  When their son was born, they **had been** married for three years. *(past perfect)*

Unit 24 - Will be doing and will have done - exercises

24.1 Read about Colin. Then tick (✓) the sentences which are true. In each group of sentences at least one is true.

Colin goes to work every day. He leaves home at 8 o'clock and arrives at work at about 8.45. He starts work immediately and continues until 12.30 when he has lunch (which takes about half an hour). He starts work again at 1.15 and goes home at exactly 4.30. Every day he follows the same routine and tomorrow will be no exception.

1 At 7.45
   a he'll be leaving the house
   b he'll have left the house
   c he'll be at home ✓
   d he'll be having breakfast ✓

4 At 12.45
   a he'll have lunch
   b he'll be having lunch
   c he'll have finished his lunch
   d he'll have started his lunch

2 At 8.15
   a he'll be leaving the house
   b he'll have left the house
   c he'll have arrived at work
   d he'll be arriving at work

5 At 4 o'clock
   a he'll have finished work
   b he'll finish work
   c he'll be working
   d he won't have finished work

3 At 9.15
   a he'll be working
   b he'll start work
   c he'll have started work
   d he'll be arriving at work

6 At 4.45
   a he'll leave work
   b he'll be leaving work
   c he'll have left work
   d he'll have arrived home

24.2 Put the verb into the correct form, will be (do)ing or will have (done).

1 Don't phone between 7 and 8. _We'll be having_ (we / have) dinner then.
2 Phone me after 8 o'clock. .... (we / finish) dinner by then.
3 Tomorrow afternoon we're going to play tennis from 3 o'clock until 4.30. So at 4 o'clock,
.... (we / play) tennis.
4 A: Can we meet tomorrow?
  B: Yes, but not in the afternoon. .... (I / work).
5 B has to go to a meeting which begins at 10 o'clock. It will last about an hour.
  A: Will you be free at 11.30?
  B: Yes, ... (the meeting / end) by then.
6 Ben is on holiday and he is spending his money very quickly. If he continues like this,
.... (he / spend) all his money before the end of his
holiday.
7 Do you think .... (you / still / do) the same job in
ten years' time?
8 Lisa is from New Zealand. She is travelling around Europe at the moment. So far she has
travelled about 1,000 miles. By the end of the trip, ...
(she / travel) more than 3,000 miles.
9 If you need to contact me, ... (I / stay) at the Lion Hotel
until Friday.
10 A: .... (you / see) Laura tomorrow?
   B: Yes, probably. Why?
   A: I borrowed this CD from her. Can you give it back to her?

Unit 25 - When I do/When I've done/When and if - lesson

Study this example:

> Will you phone me tomorrow?

> Yes, I'll phone you **when I get** home from work.

'I'll phone you when I get home' is a sentence with two parts:

> *the main part*: 'I'll phone you'
> and *the when-part*: 'when I get home'

The time in the sentence is future ('tomorrow'), but we use a *present* tense (I get) in the **when**-part of the sentence.

We do *not* use **will** in the **when**-part of the sentence.

Some more examples:
- We'll go out **when** it **stops** raining. (*not* when it will stop)
- **When** you **are** in London again, come and see us. (*not* When you will be)
- (*said to a child*) What do you want to be **when** you **grow** up? (*not* will grow)

The same thing happens after **while / before / after / as soon as / until** or **till**:
- I'm going to read a lot **while I'm** on holiday. (*not* while I will be)
- I'll probably go back home on Sunday. **Before I go**, I'd like to visit the museum.
- Wait here **until** (*or* **till**) I **come** back.

You can also use the present perfect (**have done**) after **when / after / until / as soon as**:
- Can I borrow that book **when** you've **finished** with it?
- Don't say anything while Ian is here. Wait **until** he **has gone**.

If you use the present perfect, one thing must be complete *before* the other (so the two things do *not* happen together):
- **When I've phoned** Kate, we can have dinner.
  (= First I'll phone Kate and *after that* we can have dinner.)

Do not use the present perfect if the two things happen together:
- **When I phone** Kate, I'll ask her about the party. (*not* When I've phoned)

It is often possible to use either the present simple or the present perfect:
- I'll come **as soon as I finish**.   *or*   I'll come **as soon as I've finished**.
- You'll feel better **after you have** something to eat   *or*   You'll feel better **after you've had** something to eat.

After **if**, we normally use the present simple (**if I do / if I see** etc.) for the future:
- It's raining hard. We'll get wet **if** we **go** out. (*not* if we will go)
- I'll be angry **if** it **happens** again. (*not* if it will happen)
- Hurry up! **If** we **don't** hurry, we'll be late.

Compare **when** and **if**:

We use **when** for things which are *sure* to happen:
- I'm going shopping later. (for sure) **When** I go shopping, I'll buy some food.

We use **if** (*not* when) for things that will *possibly* happen:
- I might go shopping later. (it's possible) **If** I go shopping, I'll buy some food.
- **If** it is raining this evening, I won't go out. (*not* When it is raining)
- Don't worry **if** I'm late tonight. (*not* when I'm late)
- **If** they don't come soon, I'm not going to wait. (*not* When they don't come)

Unit 25 - When I do/When I've done/When and if - exercises

25.1 Complete the sentences using the verbs in brackets. All the sentences are about the future. Use **will/won't** or the present simple (I **see** / he **plays** / it **is** etc.).

1 I _'ll phone_ (phone) you when I _get_ (get) home from work.
2 I want to see Julia before she .... (go) out.
3 We're going on holiday tomorrow. I .... (tell) you all about it when we .... (come) back.
4 Brian looks very different now. When you .... (see) him again, you .... (not / recognise) him.
5 .... (you / be) lonely without me while I .... (be) away?
6 We must do something soon before it .... (be) too late.
7 I don't want to go without you. I .... (wait) until you .... (be) ready.
8 Sue has applied for the job, but she isn't very well-qualified for it. I .... (be) surprised if she .... (get) it.
9 I hope to play tennis tomorrow if the weather .... (be) nice.
10 I'm going out now. If anybody .... (phone) while I .... (be) out, can you take a message?

25.2 Make one sentence from two.

1 It will stop raining soon. Then we'll go out.
   We'll go out .... when _it stops raining._
2 I'll find somewhere to live. Then I'll give you my address.
   I .... when ....
3 I'll do the shopping. Then I'll come straight back home.
   .... after ....
4 It's going to get dark. Let's go home before that.
   .... before ....
5 She must apologise to me first. I won't speak to her until then.
   .... until ....

25.3 Read the situations and complete the sentences.

1 A friend of yours is going on holiday. You want to know what she is going to do.
   You ask: What are you going to do when _you are on holiday_ ?
2 A friend of yours is visiting you. She has to go soon but maybe there's time for some more coffee.
   You ask: Would you like some more coffee before .... ?
3 You want to sell your car. Jim is interested in buying it, but he hasn't decided yet.
   You ask: Can you let me know as soon as .... ?
4 Your friends are going to New York soon. You want to know where they're going to stay.
   You ask: Where are you going to stay when .... ?
5 The traffic is very bad in your town, but they are building a new road at the moment.
   You say: I think things will be better when they ....

25.4 Put in **when** or **if**.

1 Don't worry _if_ I'm late tonight.
2 Tom might phone while I'm out this evening. .... he does, can you take a message?
3 I'm going to Rome next week. .... I'm there, I hope to visit a friend of mine.
4 I think Jill will get the job. I'll be very surprised .... she doesn't get it.
5 I'm going shopping. .... you want anything, I can get it for you.
6 I'm going away for a few days. I'll phone you .... I get back.
7 I want you to come to the party, but .... you don't want to come, that's all right.
8 We can eat at home or, ... you prefer, we can go to a restaurant.

Unit 26 - Can, could and (be) able to - lesson

We use **can** to say that something is possible or allowed, or that somebody has the ability to do something. We use **can** + *infinitive* (**can do** / **can see** etc.):
- □ We **can see** the lake from our bedroom window.
- □ 'I haven't got a pen.' 'You **can use** mine.'
- □ **Can** you **speak** any foreign languages?
- □ I **can come** and see you tomorrow if you like.
- □ The word 'play' **can be** a noun or a verb.

The negative is **can't** (= **cannot**):
- □ I'm afraid I **can't come** to the party on Friday.

You can say that somebody is **able to** do something, but **can** is more usual:
- □ We **are able to see** the lake from our bedroom window.

But **can** has only two forms: **can** (*present*) and **could** (*past*). So sometimes it is necessary to use (be) **able to**. Compare:

□ I **can't** sleep.	□ I **haven't been able to** sleep recently.
□ Tom **can come** tomorrow.	□ Tom **might be able to** come tomorrow.
□ Maria **can speak** French, Spanish and English.	□ Applicants for the job **must be able to** speak two foreign languages.

Could

Sometimes **could** is the past of **can**. We use **could** especially with:

see hear smell taste feel remember understand
- □ We had a lovely room in the hotel. We **could see** the lake.
- □ As soon as I walked into the room, I **could smell** gas.
- □ I was sitting at the back of the theatre and **couldn't hear** very well.

We also use **could** to say that somebody had the general ability or permission to do something:
- □ My grandfather **could speak** five languages.
- □ We were totally free. We **could do** what we wanted. (= we were allowed to do)

Could and was able to

We use **could** for *general* ability. But if you want to say that somebody did something in a specific situation, use **was/were able to** or **managed to** (*not* could):
- □ The fire spread through the building very quickly, but fortunately everybody **was able to escape** / **managed to escape**. (*not* could escape)
- □ We didn't know where David was, but we **managed to find** / **were able to find** him in the end. (*not* could find)

Compare:
- □ Mike was an excellent tennis player when he was younger. He **could beat** anybody. (= he had the general ability to beat anybody)
- *but* Mike and Pete played tennis yesterday. Pete played very well, but Mike **managed to beat** him. (= he managed to beat him in this particular game)

The negative **couldn't** (**could not**) is possible in all situations:
- □ My grandfather **couldn't swim**.
- □ We looked for David everywhere, but we **couldn't find** him.
- □ Pete played well, but he **couldn't beat** Mike.

Unit 26 - Can, could and (be) able to - exercises

26.1 Complete the sentences using **can** or **(be) able to**. Use **can** if possible; otherwise use **(be) able to**.

1 Gary has travelled a lot. He ___can___ speak five languages.
2 I haven't ___been able to___ sleep very well recently.
3 Nicole _____ drive, but she hasn't got a car.
4 I used to _____ stand on my head, but I can't do it now.
5 I can't understand Martin. I've never _____ understand him.
6 I can't see you on Friday, but I _____ meet you on Saturday morning.
7 Ask Catherine about your problem. She might _____ help you.

26.2 Write sentences about yourself using the ideas in brackets.

1 (something you used to be able to do)
   I used to be able to sing well.
2 (something you used to be able to do)
   I used _____
3 (something you would like to be able to do)
   I'd _____
4 (something you have never been able to do)
   I've _____

26.3 Complete the sentences with **can/can't/could/couldn't** + the following:

   ~~come~~   eat   hear   run   sleep   wait

1 I'm afraid I ___can't come___ to your party next week.
2 When Tim was 16, he _____ 100 metres in 11 seconds.
3 'Are you in a hurry?'   'No, I've got plenty of time. I _____ .'
4 I was feeling sick yesterday. I _____ anything.
5 Can you speak a little louder? I _____ you very well.
6 'You look tired.'   'Yes, I _____ last night.'

26.4 Complete the answers to the questions with **was/were able to** ... .

1 A: Did everybody escape from the fire?
   B: Yes, although the fire spread quickly, everybody ___was able to escape___ .
2 A: Did you finish your work this afternoon?
   B: Yes, there was nobody to disturb me, so I _____ .
3 A: Did you have difficulty finding our house?
   B: Not really. Your directions were good and we _____ .
4 A: Did the thief get away?
   B: Yes. No-one realised what was happening and the thief _____ .

26.5 Complete the sentences using **could, couldn't** or **managed to**.

1 My grandfather travelled a lot. He ___could___ speak five languages.
2 I looked everywhere for the book, but I ___couldn't___ find it.
3 They didn't want to come with us at first, but we ___managed to___ persuade them.
4 Laura had hurt her leg and _____ walk very well.
5 Sue wasn't at home when I phoned, but I _____ contact her at her office.
6 I looked very carefully and I _____ see somebody in the distance.
7 I wanted to buy some tomatoes. The first shop I went to didn't have any, but I _____ get some in the next shop.
8 My grandmother loved music. She _____ play the piano very well.
9 A girl fell into the river, but fortunately we _____ rescue her.
10 I had forgotten to bring my camera, so I _____ take any photographs.

Unit 27 - Could (do) and could have (done) - lesson

We use **could** in a number of ways. Sometimes **could** is the past of **can** (see Unit 26):
- ☐ Listen. I **can hear** something. *(now)*
- ☐ I listened. I **could hear** something. *(past)*

But **could** is not only used in this way. We also use **could** to talk about possible actions *now* or *in the future* (especially to make suggestions).
For example:
- ☐ A: What shall we do this evening?
  B: We **could go** to the cinema.
- ☐ A: When you go to Paris next month, you **could stay** with Julia.
  B: Yes, I suppose I **could**.

> What shall we do this evening?

> We could go to the cinema.

Can is also possible in these sentences ('We **can** go to the cinema.' etc.). With **could**, the suggestion is less sure.

We also use **could** (*not* **can**) for actions which are not realistic. For example:
- ☐ I'm so tired, I **could sleep** for a week. (*not* I can sleep for a week)

Compare **can** and **could**:
- ☐ I **can stay** with Julia when I go to Paris. (realistic)
- ☐ Maybe I **could stay** with Julia when I go to Paris. (possible, but less sure)
- ☐ This is a wonderful place. I **could stay** here for ever. (unrealistic)

We also use **could** (*not* **can**) to say that something is possible now or in the future. The meaning is similar to **might** or **may** (see Unit 29):
- ☐ The story **could be** true, but I don't think it is. (*not* can be true)
- ☐ I don't know what time Liz is coming. She **could get** here at any time.

We use **could have** (done) to talk about the past. Compare:
- ☐ I'm so tired, I **could sleep** for a week. *(now)*
  I was so tired, I **could have slept** for a week. *(past)*
- ☐ The situation is bad, but it **could be** worse. *(now)*
  The situation was bad, but it **could have been** worse. *(past)*

Something **could have** happened = it was possible but did *not* happen:
- ☐ Why did you stay at a hotel when you were in Paris? You **could have stayed** with Julia. (you didn't stay with her)
- ☐ I didn't know that you wanted to go to the concert. I **could have got** you a ticket. (I didn't get you a ticket)
- ☐ Dave was lucky. He **could have hurt** himself when he fell, but he's OK.

We use **couldn't** to say that something would not be possible now:
- ☐ I **couldn't live** in a big city. I'd hate it. (= it wouldn't be possible for me)
- ☐ Everything is fine right now. Things **couldn't be** better.

For the past we use **couldn't have** (done):
- ☐ We had a really good holiday. It **couldn't have been** better.
- ☐ The trip was cancelled last week. Paul **couldn't have gone** anyway because he was ill. (= it would not have been possible for him to go)

58

Unit 27 - Could (do) and could have (done) - exercises

27.1 Answer the questions with a suggestion. Use **could**.

1 Where shall we go for our holidays?	(to Scotland) _We could go to Scotland._
2 What shall we have for dinner tonight?	(fish) We ....
3 When shall I phone Angela?	(now) You ....
4 What shall I give Ann for her birthday?	(a book) ....
5 Where shall we hang this picture?	(in the kitchen) ....

27.2 In some of these sentences, you need **could** (not **can**). Change the sentences where necessary.

1 The story can be true, but I don't think it is. _could be true_
2 It's a nice day. We can go for a walk. _OK (could go is also possible)_
3 I'm so angry with him. I can kill him! ....
4 If you're hungry, we can have dinner now. ....
5 It's so nice here. I can stay here all day, but ....
  unfortunately I have to go.
6 A: Where's my bag. Have you seen it?
  B: No, but it can be in the car. ....
7 Peter is a keen musician. He plays the flute and ....
  he can also play the piano.
8 A: I need to borrow a camera.
  B: You can borrow mine.
9 The weather is nice now, but it can change later. ....

27.3 Complete the sentences. Use **could** or **could have** + a suitable verb.

1 A: What shall we do this evening?
  B: I don't mind. We _could go_ to the cinema.
2 A: I had a very boring evening at home yesterday.
  B: Why did you stay at home? You .... out with us.
3 A: There's an interesting job advertised in the paper. You .... for it.
  B: What sort of job? Show me the advertisement.
4 A: How was your exam? Was it difficult?
  B: It wasn't so bad. It .... worse.
5 A: I got very wet walking home in the rain last night.
  B: Why did you walk? You .... a taxi.
6 A: Where shall we meet tomorrow?
  B: Well, I .... to your house if you like.

27.4 Complete the sentences. Use **couldn't** or **couldn't have** + these verbs (in the correct form):

  ~~be~~   be   come   find   get   ~~live~~   wear

1 I _couldn't live_ in a big city. I'd hate it.
2 We had a really good holiday. It _couldn't have been_ better.
3 I .... that hat. I'd look silly and people would laugh at me.
4 We managed to find the restaurant you recommended, but we .... it
  without the map that you drew for us.
5 Paul has to get up at 4 o'clock every morning. I don't know how he does it. I
  .... up at that time every day.
6 The staff at the hotel were really nice when we stayed there last summer. They
  .... more helpful.
7 A: I tried to phone you last week. We had a party and I wanted to invite you.
  B: That was nice of you, but I .... anyway. I was away all last week.

Unit 28 - Must and can't - lesson

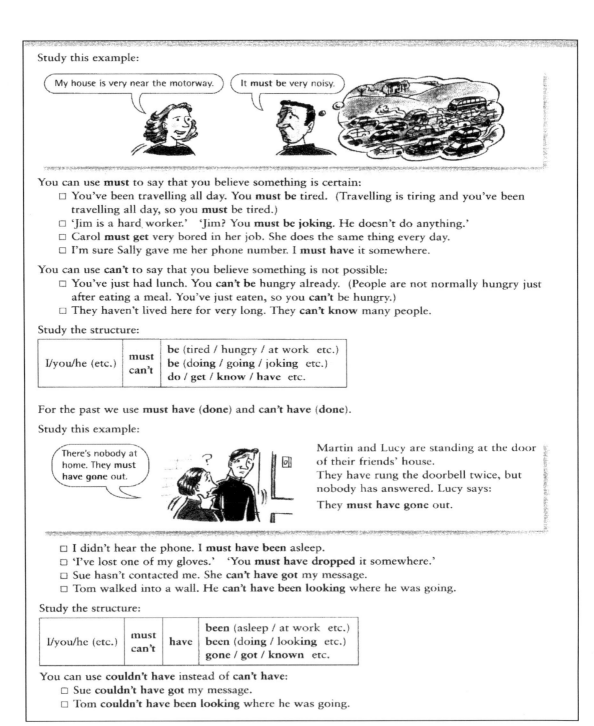

Study this example:

You can use **must** to say that you believe something is certain:
- ☐ You've been travelling all day. You **must be** tired. (Travelling is tiring and you've been travelling all day, so you **must** be tired.)
- ☐ 'Jim is a hard worker.' 'Jim? You **must be joking**. He doesn't do anything.'
- ☐ Carol **must get** very bored in her job. She does the same thing every day.
- ☐ I'm sure Sally gave me her phone number. I **must have** it somewhere.

You can use **can't** to say that you believe something is not possible:
- ☐ You've just had lunch. You **can't be** hungry already. (People are not normally hungry just after eating a meal. You've just eaten, so you **can't** be hungry.)
- ☐ They haven't lived here for very long. They **can't know** many people.

Study the structure:

I/you/he (etc.)	must can't	be (tired / hungry / at work etc.) be (doing / going / joking etc.) do / get / know / have etc.

For the past we use **must have (done)** and **can't have (done)**.

Study this example:

Martin and Lucy are standing at the door of their friends' house.
They have rung the doorbell twice, but nobody has answered. Lucy says:
They **must have gone** out.

- ☐ I didn't hear the phone. I **must have been** asleep.
- ☐ 'I've lost one of my gloves.' 'You **must have dropped** it somewhere.'
- ☐ Sue hasn't contacted me. She **can't have got** my message.
- ☐ Tom walked into a wall. He **can't have been looking** where he was going.

Study the structure:

I/you/he (etc.)	must can't	have	been (asleep / at work etc.) been (doing / looking etc.) gone / got / known etc.

You can use **couldn't have** instead of **can't have**:
- ☐ Sue **couldn't have got** my message.
- ☐ Tom **couldn't have been looking** where he was going.

Unit 28 - Must and can't - exercises

28.1 Put in **must** or **can't**.

1 You've been travelling all day. You ___must___ be tired.
2 That restaurant .... be very good. It's always full of people.
3 That restaurant .... be very good. It's always empty.
4 I'm sure I gave you the key. You .... have it. Have you looked in your bag?
5 You're going on holiday next week. You .... be looking forward to it.
6 It rained every day during their holiday, so they .... have had a very nice time.
7 Congratulations on passing your exam. You .... be very pleased.
8 You got here very quickly. You .... have walked very fast.
9 Bill and Sue always travel business class, so they .... be short of money.

28.2 Complete each sentence with a verb (one or two words) in the correct form.

1 I've lost one of my gloves. I must ___have dropped___ it somewhere.
2 They haven't lived here for very long. They can't ___know___ many people.
3 Ted isn't at work today. He must .... ill.
4 Ted wasn't at work last week. He must .... ill.
5 *(the doorbell rings)* I wonder who that is. It can't .... Mary. She's still at work at this time.
6 Sarah knows a lot about films. She must .... to the cinema a lot.
7 Look. James is putting on his hat and coat. He must .... out.
8 I left my bike outside the house last night and now it has gone. Somebody must .... it.
9 Amy was in a very difficult situation when she lost her job. It can't .... easy for her.
10 There is a man walking behind us. He has been walking behind us for the last twenty minutes. He must .... us.

28.3 Read the situations and use the words in brackets to write sentences with **must have** and **can't have**.

1 The phone rang, but I didn't hear it. (I / asleep)
   I must have been asleep.
2 Sue hasn't contacted me. (she / get / my message)
   She can't have got my message.
3 The jacket you bought is very good quality. (it / very expensive)
   ....
4 I haven't seen the people next door for ages. (they / go away)
   ....
5 I can't find my umbrella. (I / leave / it in the restaurant last night)
   ....
6 Dave, who is usually very friendly, walked past me without speaking. (he / see / me)
   ....
7 There was a man standing outside the café. (he / wait / for somebody)
   ....
8 Liz did the opposite of what I asked her to do. (she / understand / what I said)
   ....
9 When I got back to my car, the door was unlocked. (I / forget / to lock it)
   ....
10 I was woken up in the night by the noise next door. (the neighbours / have / a party)
   ....
11 The light was red, but the car didn't stop. (the driver / see / the red light)
   ....

Unit 29 - May and might 1 - lesson

Study this example situation:

You are looking for Bob. Nobody is sure where he is, but you get some suggestions.

Where's Bob?	He **may** be in his office.	(= perhaps he is in his office)
	He **might** be having lunch.	(= perhaps he is having lunch)
	Ask Ann. She **might** know.	(= perhaps she knows)

We use **may** or **might** to say that something is a possibility. Usually you can use **may** or **might**, so you can say:

☐ It **may** be true. *or* It **might** be true. (= perhaps it is true)
☐ She **might** know. *or* She **may** know.

The negative forms are **may not** and **might not** (*or* **mightn't**):

☐ It **may not** be true. (= perhaps it isn't true)
☐ She **might not** work here any more. (= perhaps she doesn't work here)

Study the structure:

I/you/he (etc.)	may might	(not)	be (true / in his office etc.) be (doing / working / having etc.) know / work / want etc.

For the past we use **may have (done)** or **might have (done)**:

☐ A: I wonder why Kate didn't answer the phone.
  B: She **may have been** asleep. (= perhaps she was asleep)
☐ A: I can't find my bag anywhere.
  B: You **might have left** it in the shop. (= perhaps you left it in the shop)
☐ A: I was surprised that Kate wasn't at the meeting yesterday.
  B: She **might not have known** about it. (= perhaps she didn't know)
☐ A: I wonder why David was in such a bad mood yesterday.
  B: He **may not have been feeling** well. (= perhaps he wasn't feeling well)

Study the structure:

I/you/he (etc.)	may might	(not) have	been (asleep / at home etc.) been (doing / working / feeling etc.) known / had / wanted / left etc.

Could is similar to **may** and **might**:

☐ It's a strange story, but it **could** be true. (= it may/might be true)
☐ You **could have left** your bag in the shop. (= you may/might have left it)

But **couldn't** (*negative*) is different from **may not** and **might not**. Compare:

☐ Sarah **couldn't have** got my message. Otherwise she would have replied.
  (= it is not possible that she got my message)
☐ I wonder why Sarah hasn't replied to my message. I suppose she **might not have** got it.
  (= perhaps she didn't get it, and perhaps she did)

Unit 29 - May and might 1 - exercises

29.1 Write these sentences in a different way using **might**.

1 Perhaps Helen is in her office.   _She might be in her office._
2 Perhaps Helen is busy.
3 Perhaps she is working.
4 Perhaps she wants to be alone.
5 Perhaps she was ill yesterday.
6 Perhaps she went home early.
7 Perhaps she had to go home early.
8 Perhaps she was working yesterday.

In sentences 9–11 use **might not**.

9 Perhaps she doesn't want to see me.
10 Perhaps she isn't working today.
11 Perhaps she wasn't feeling well yesterday.

29.2 Complete each sentence with a verb in the correct form.

1 'Where's Sam?' 'I'm not sure. He might _be having_ lunch.'
2 'Who is that man with Emily?' 'I'm not sure. It might _____ her brother.'
3 A: Who was the man we saw with Anna yesterday?
  B: I'm not sure. It may _____ her brother.
4 A: What are those people doing by the side of the road?
  B: I don't know. They might _____ for a bus.
5 'Do you have a stamp?' 'No, but ask Simon. He may _____ one.'

29.3 Read the situation and make sentences from the words in brackets. Use **might**.

1 I can't find Jeff anywhere. I wonder where he is.
  a (he / go / shopping) _He might have gone shopping._
  b (he / play / tennis) _He might be playing tennis._
2 I'm looking for Sarah. Do you know where she is?
  a (she / watch / TV / in her room) _____
  b (she / go / out) _____
3 I can't find my umbrella. Have you seen it?
  a (it / be / in the car) _____
  b (you / leave / in the restaurant last night) _____
4 Why didn't Dave answer the doorbell? I'm sure he was at home at the time.
  a (he / go / to bed early) _____
  b (he / not / hear / the doorbell) _____
  c (he / be / in the shower) _____

29.4 Complete the sentences using **might not have …** or **couldn't have …** .

1 A: Do you think Sarah got the message we sent her?
  B: No, she would have contacted us. _She couldn't have got it_ .
2 A: I was surprised Kate wasn't at the meeting. Perhaps she didn't know about it.
  B: That's possible. _She might not have known about it_ .
3 A: I wonder why they never replied to our letter. Do you think they received it?
  B: Maybe not. They _____ .
4 A: I wonder how the fire started. Was it an accident?
  B: No, the police say it _____ .
5 A: Mike says he needs to see you. He tried to find you yesterday.
  B: Well, he _____ very hard. I was in my office all day.
6 A: The man you spoke to – are you sure he was American?
  B: No, I'm not sure. He _____ .

Unit 30 - May and might 2 - lesson

We use **may** and **might** to talk about possible actions or happenings in the future:
- ☐ I haven't decided yet where to go for my holidays. I **may go** to Ireland. (= perhaps I will go there)
- ☐ Take an umbrella with you. It **might rain** later. (= perhaps it will rain)
- ☐ The bus isn't always on time. We **might have** to wait a few minutes. (= perhaps we will have to wait)

The negative forms are **may not** and **might not** (**mightn't**):
- ☐ Liz **may not go** out tonight. She isn't feeling well. (= perhaps she will not go out)
- ☐ There **might not be** enough time to discuss everything at the meeting. (= perhaps there will not be enough time)

Compare **will** and **may/might**:
- ☐ I'll **be** late this evening. (for sure)
- ☐ I **may/might** be late this evening. (possible)

Usually you can use **may** or **might**. So you can say:
- ☐ I **may go** to Ireland. *or* I **might go** to Ireland.
- ☐ Jane **might be** able to help you. *or* Jane **may be** able to help you.

But we use only **might** (*not* may) when the situation is *not real*:
- ☐ If I were in Tom's position, I **might** look for another job.
The situation here is not real because I am *not* in Tom's position (so I'm not going to look for another job). **May** is not possible in this example.

There is also a continuous form: **may/might be -ing**. Compare this with **will be -ing**:
- ☐ Don't phone at 8.30. I'll **be watching** the film on television.
- ☐ Don't phone at 8.30. I **might be watching** (or I **may be watching**) the film on television. (= perhaps I'll be watching it)

We also use **may/might be -ing** for possible plans. Compare:
- ☐ I'm **going** to Ireland in July. (for sure)
- ☐ I **may be going** (or I **might be going**) to Ireland in July. (possible)
But you can also say 'I **may go** (or I **might go**) ...' with little difference in meaning.

Might as well

Rose and Clare have just missed the bus. The buses run every hour.

What shall we do? Shall we walk?

We **might as well**. It's a nice day and I don't want to wait here for an hour.

We **might as well** do something = We should do it because there is no better alternative. There is no reason not to do it.

May as well is also possible.

- ☐ A: What time are you going out?
  B: Well, I'm ready, so I **might as well** go now.
- ☐ Buses are so expensive these days, you **may as well** get a taxi. (= taxis are as good, no more expensive)

Unit 30 - May and might 2 - exercises

30.1 Write sentences with **might**.

1 Where are you going for your holidays? (to Ireland???)
I haven't decided yet. *I might go to Ireland.*

2 What sort of car are you going to buy? (a Mercedes???)
I'm not sure yet. I

3 What are you doing this weekend? (go to London???)
I haven't decided yet.

4 When is Tom coming to see us? (on Saturday???)
He hasn't said yet.

5 Where are you going to hang that picture? (in the dining room???)
I haven't made up my mind yet.

6 What is Julia going to do when she leaves school? (go to university???)
She's still thinking about it.

30.2 Complete the sentences using **might** + the following:

bite   break   need   ~~rain~~   slip   wake

1 Take an umbrella with you when you go out. It ____might rain____ later.
2 Don't make too much noise. You _____ the baby.
3 Be careful of that dog. It _____ you.
4 I don't think we should throw that letter away. We _____ it later.
5 Be careful. The footpath is very icy. You _____ .
6 Don't let the children play in this room. They _____ something.

30.3 Complete the sentences using **might be able to** or **might have to** + a suitable verb.

1 I can't help you, but why don't you ask Jane? She ____might be able to help____ you.
2 I can't meet you this evening, but I _____ you tomorrow.
3 I'm not working on Saturday, but I _____ on Sunday.
4 I can come to the meeting, but I _____ before the end.

30.4 Write sentences with **might not**.

1 I'm not sure that Liz will come to the party.
Liz might not come to the party.

2 I'm not sure that I'll go out this evening.
I _____

3 I'm not sure that we'll get tickets for the concert.
We _____

4 I'm not sure that Sue will be able to come out with us this evening.
_____

30.5 Read the situations and make sentences with **might as well**.

1 You and a friend have just missed the bus. The buses run every hour.
You say: We'll have to wait an hour for the next bus. *We might as well walk.*

2 You have a free ticket for a concert. You're not very keen on the concert, but you decide to go.
You say: I _____ to the concert. It's a pity to waste a free ticket.

3 You've just painted your kitchen. You still have a lot of paint, so why not paint the bathroom too?
You say: We _____ . There's plenty of paint left.

4 You and a friend are at home. You're bored. There's a film on TV starting in a few minutes.
You say: _____ There's nothing else to do.

Unit 31 - Have to and must - lesson

I **have to** do something = it is necessary to do it, I am obliged to do it:
- ☐ You can't turn right here. You **have to turn** left.
- ☐ I **have to wear** glasses for reading.
- ☐ George can't come out with us this evening. He **has to work** late.
- ☐ Last week Tina broke her arm and **had to go** to hospital.
- ☐ I haven't **had to go** to the doctor for ages.

> You have to turn left here.

We use **do/does/did** in questions and negative sentences (for the present and past simple):
- ☐ What **do** I **have to do** to get a new driving licence? (*not* What have I to do?)
- ☐ Karen **doesn't have to work** Saturdays. (*not* Karen hasn't to)
- ☐ Why **did** you **have to leave** early?

You can use **have to** with **will** and **might/may**:
- ☐ If the pain gets worse, you**'ll have to go** to the doctor.
- ☐ I **might have to work** late tomorrow evening. *or* I **may have to work** …
  (= it's possible that I will have to)

Must is similar to **have to**:
- ☐ It's later than I thought. I **must go**. *or* I **have to go**.

You can use **must** to give your own opinion (for example, to say what *you* think is necessary, or to recommend someone to do something). **Have to** is also possible:
- ☐ I haven't spoken to Sue for ages. I **must phone** her. (= I say this is necessary)
- ☐ Mark is a really nice person. You **must meet** him. (I recommend this)

We use **have to** (*not* **must**) to say what someone is *obliged* to do. The speaker is not giving his/her own opinion:
- ☐ I **have to work** from 8.30 to 5.30 every day. (a fact, not an opinion)
- ☐ Jane **has to travel** a lot for her work.

But **must** is often used in written rules and instructions:
- ☐ Applications for the job **must be received** by 18 May.
- ☐ *(exam instruction)* You **must write** your answers in ink.

You cannot use **must** to talk about the past:
- ☐ We **had** to leave early. (*not* we must)

Mustn't and **don't have to** are completely different:

You **mustn't** do something = it is necessary that you do *not* do it (so don't do it):	You **don't have to** do something = you don't need to do it (but you can if you want):
☐ You **must keep** it a secret. You **mustn't tell** anyone. (= don't tell anyone)	☐ You **don't have to tell** him, but you can if you want to.
☐ I promised I would be on time. I **mustn't be** late. (= I must be on time)	☐ I **don't have to be** at the meeting, but I think I'll go anyway.

You can use **have got to** instead of **have to**. So you can say:
- ☐ I**'ve got to** work tomorrow.   *or*   I **have to** work tomorrow.
- ☐ When **has** Liz **got to** go?   *or*   When **does** Liz **have to** go?

Unit 31 - Have to and must - exercises

31.1 Complete the sentences with **have to / has to / had to**.

1 Bill starts work at 5 a.m. ___He has to get up___ at four. (he / get up)
2 'I broke my arm last week.' '___Did you have to go___ to hospital?' (you / go)
3 There was a lot of noise from the street. _____ the window. (we / close)
4 Karen can't stay for the whole meeting. _____ early. (she / leave)
5 How old _____ to drive in your country? (you / be)
6 I don't have much time. _____. (I / hurry)
7 How is Paul enjoying his new job? _____ a lot? (he / travel)
8 'I'm afraid I can't stay long.' 'What time _____?' (you / go)
9 'The bus was late again.' 'How long _____?' (you / wait)
10 There was nobody to help me. I _____ everything by myself. (I / do)

31.2 Complete the sentences using **have to** + the verbs in the list. Some sentences are positive (**I have to** ... etc.) and some are negative (**I don't have to** ... etc.):

    ask   do   drive   ~~get up~~   go   make   make   pay   ~~show~~

1 I'm not working tomorrow, so I ___don't have to get up___ early.
2 Steve didn't know how to use the computer, so I ___had to show___ him.
3 Excuse me a moment – I _____ a phone call. I won't be long.
4 I'm not so busy. I have a few things to do, but I _____ them now.
5 I couldn't find the street I wanted. I _____ somebody for directions.
6 The car park is free. You _____ to park your car there.
7 A man was injured in the accident, but he _____ to hospital because it wasn't serious.
8 Sue has a senior position in the company. She _____ important decisions.
9 When Patrick starts his new job next month, he _____ 50 miles to work every day.

31.3 In some of these sentences, **must** is wrong or unnatural. Correct the sentences where necessary.

1 It's later than I thought. I must go.	OK (have to *is also correct*)
2 I must work every day from 8.30 to 5.30.	I have to work
3 You must come and see us again soon.	_____
4 Tom can't meet us tomorrow. He must work.	_____
5 I must work late yesterday evening.	_____
6 I must get up early tomorrow. I have lots to do.	_____
7 Julia wears glasses. She must wear glasses since she was very young.	_____

31.4 Complete the sentences with **mustn't** or **don't/doesn't have to**.

1 I don't want anyone to know about our plan. You ___mustn't___ tell anyone.
2 Richard ___doesn't have to___ wear a suit to work, but he usually does.
3 I can stay in bed tomorrow morning because I _____ go to work.
4 Whatever you do, you _____ touch that switch. It's very dangerous.
5 There's a lift in the building, so we _____ climb the stairs.
6 You _____ forget what I told you. It's very important.
7 Sue _____ get up early, but she usually does.
8 Don't make so much noise. We _____ wake the children.
9 I _____ eat too much. I'm supposed to be on a diet.
10 You _____ be a good player to enjoy a game of tennis.

Unit 32 - Must/mustn't/needn't - lesson

Must   mustn't   needn't

You **must** do something = it is necessary that you do it:
- □ Don't tell anybody what I said. You **must** keep it a secret.
- □ We haven't got much time. We **must** hurry.

You **mustn't** do something = it is necessary that you do *not* do it (so don't do it):
- □ You **must** keep it a secret. You **mustn't** tell anybody else. (= don't tell anybody else)
- □ We **must** be very quiet. We **mustn't** make any noise.

You **needn't** do something = you don't need to do it (but you can if you like):
- □ You can come with me if you like, but you **needn't come** if you don't want to. (= it is not necessary for you to come)
- □ We've got plenty of time. We **needn't hurry**. (= it is not necessary to hurry)

Instead of **needn't**, you can use **don't/doesn't need to**. So you can say:
- □ We **needn't** hurry. *or* We **don't need to** hurry.

Remember that we say **don't need to do**, but **needn't do** (*without* to).

Needn't have (done)

Study this example situation:

Paul had to go out. He thought it was going to rain, so he took the umbrella.

But it didn't rain, so the umbrella was not necessary. So he **needn't have taken** it.

He **needn't have taken** the umbrella = He took the umbrella, but this was not necessary.

Compare **needn't** (do) and **needn't have** (done):
- □ Everything will be OK. You **needn't worry**. (it's not necessary)
- □ Everything was OK. You **needn't have worried**. (you worried, but it was not necessary)

Didn't need to (do) and **needn't have** (done)

I **didn't need to** ... = it was not necessary for me to ... (and I knew this at the time):
- □ I **didn't need** to get up early, so I didn't.
- □ I **didn't need** to get up early, but it was a lovely morning, so I did.

I **didn't have to** ... is also possible in these examples.

I **needn't have done** something = I did it, but *now I know* that it was not necessary:
- □ I got up very early because I had to get ready to go away. But in fact it didn't take me long to get ready. So, I **needn't have got** up so early. I could have stayed in bed longer.

Unit 32 - Must/mustn't/needn't - exercises

32.1 Complete the sentences using **needn't** + the following verbs:

ask   come   explain   ~~leave~~   tell   walk

1 We've got plenty of time. We _needn't leave_ yet.
2 I can manage the shopping alone. You _____ with me.
3 We _____ all the way home. We can get a taxi.
4 Just help yourself if you'd like more to eat. You _____ first.
5 We can keep this a secret between ourselves. We _____ anybody else.
6 I understand the situation perfectly. You _____ further.

32.2 Complete the sentences with **must, mustn't** or **needn't**.

1 We haven't got much time. We _must_ hurry.
2 We've got plenty of time. We _needn't_ hurry.
3 We have enough food at home, so we _____ go shopping today.
4 Gary gave me a letter to post. I _____ remember to post it.
5 Gary gave me a letter to post. I _____ forget to post it.
6 There's plenty of time for you to make up your mind. You _____ decide now.
7 You _____ wash those tomatoes. They've already been washed.
8 This is a valuable book. You _____ look after it carefully and you _____ lose it.
9 A: What sort of house do you want to buy? Something big?
    B: Well, it _____ be big – that's not so important. But it _____ have a nice garden – that's essential.

32.3 Read the situations and make sentences with **needn't have**.

1 Paul went out. He took an umbrella because he thought it was going to rain. But it didn't rain.
    He needn't have taken an umbrella.
2 Linda bought some eggs when she went shopping. When she got home, she found that she already had plenty of eggs. She _____
3 A colleague got angry with you at work. He shouted at you, which you think was unnecessary. Later you say to him: You _____
4 Brian had money problems, so he sold his car. A few days later he won some money in a lottery. He _____
5 We took a camcorder with us on holiday, but we didn't use it in the end.
    We _____
6 I thought I was going to miss my train, so I rushed to the station. But the train was late and in the end I had to wait twenty minutes. _____

32.4 Write two sentences for each situation. Use **needn't have** in the first sentence and **could have** in the second (as in the example). For **could have**, see Unit 27.

1 Why did you rush? Why didn't you take your time?
    You needn't have rushed. You could have taken your time.
2 Why did you walk home? Why didn't you take a taxi?
    _____
3 Why did you stay at a hotel? Why didn't you stay with us?
    _____
4 Why did she phone me in the middle of the night? Why didn't she wait until the morning?
    _____
    _____
5 Why did you leave without saying anything? Why didn't you say goodbye?
    _____
    _____

Unit 33 - Should 1 - lesson

You **should do** something = it is a good thing to do or the right thing to do. You can use **should** to give advice or to give an opinion:
- You look tired. You **should go** to bed.
- The government **should do** more to reduce crime.
- '**Should we invite** Susan to the party?' 'Yes, I think we **should**.'

We often use **should** with **I think / I don't think / Do you think** ... ?:
- **I think** the government **should do** more to reduce crime.
- **I don't think** you should work so hard.
- '**Do you think** I **should apply** for this job?' 'Yes, **I think you should**.'

You **shouldn't** do something = it isn't a good thing to do:
- You **shouldn't believe** everything you read in the newspapers.

Should is not as strong as **must** or **have to**:
- You **should** apologise. (= it would be a good thing to do)
- You **must** apologise. / You **have to** apologise. (= you have no alternative)

You can use **should** when something is not right or what you expect:
- I wonder where Tina is. She **should be** here by now.
  (= she isn't here yet, and this is not normal)
- The price on this packet is wrong. It **should be** £2.50, not £3.50.
- That man on the motorbike **should be wearing** a helmet.

We also use **should** to say that we expect something to happen:
- She's been studying hard for the exam, so she **should pass**. (= I expect her to pass)
- There are plenty of hotels in the town. It **shouldn't be** difficult to find somewhere to stay. (= I don't expect it to be difficult)

You **should have done** something = you didn't do it, but it would have been the right thing to do:
- You missed a great party last night. You **should have come**. Why didn't you?
  (= you didn't come, but it would have been good to come)
- I wonder why they're so late. They **should have arrived** long ago.

You **shouldn't have done** something = you did it, but it was the wrong thing to do:
- I'm feeling sick. **I shouldn't have eaten** so much. (= I ate too much)
- She **shouldn't have been listening** to our conversation. It was private.
  (= she was listening)

Compare **should** (do) and **should have** (done):
- You look tired. You **should go** to bed now.
- You went to bed very late last night. You **should have gone** to bed earlier.

Ought to ...

You can use **ought to** instead of **should** in the sentences on this page. We say 'ought to do' (with **to**):
- Do you think I **ought to apply** for this job? (= Do you think I **should apply** ... ?)
- Jack **ought not to go** to bed so late. (= Jack **shouldn't go** ...)
- It was a great party last night. You **ought to have come**.
- She's been studying hard for the exam, so she **ought to pass**.

Unit 33 - Should 1 - exercises

33.1 For each situation, write a sentence with **should** or **shouldn't** + the following:

~~go away for a few days~~   go to bed so late   look for another job
put some pictures on the walls   take a photograph   use her car so much

1 Liz needs a change.   *She should go away for a few days.*
2 Your salary is very low.   You _____
3 Jack always has difficulty getting up.   He _____
4 What a beautiful view!   You _____
5 Sue drives everywhere. She never walks.   She _____
6 Bill's room isn't very interesting. _____

33.2 Read the situations and write sentences with **I think/I don't think ... should ... .**

1 Peter and Cathy are planning to get married. You think it's a bad idea.
     I don't think they should get married.
2 Jane has a bad cold but plans to go out this evening. You don't think this is a good idea. You say to her: _____
3 Peter needs a job. He's just seen an advertisement for a job which you think would be ideal for him, but he's not sure whether to apply or not. You say to him:
I think _____
4 The government wants to increase taxes, but you don't think this is a good idea.
_____

33.3 Complete the sentences with **should (have)** + the verb in brackets.

1 Diane *should pass* the exam. She's been studying very hard. (pass)
2 You missed a great party last night. *You should have come* . (come)
3 We don't see you enough. You _____ and see us more often. (come)
4 I'm in a difficult position. What do you think I _____ ? (do)
5 I'm sorry that I didn't take your advice. I _____ what you said. (do)
6 I'm playing tennis with Jane tomorrow. She _____ – she's much better than me. (win)
7 We lost the match, but we _____ . We were the better team. (win)
8 'Is Mike here yet?' 'Not yet, but he _____ here soon.' (be)
9 I posted the letter three days ago, so it _____ by now. (arrive)

33.4 Read the situations and write sentences with **should/shouldn't**. Some of the sentences are past and some are present.

1 I'm feeling sick. I ate too much.   *I shouldn't have eaten so much.*
2 That man on the motorbike isn't wearing a helmet. That's dangerous.
He *should be wearing a helmet.*
3 When we got to the restaurant, there were no free tables. We hadn't reserved one.
We _____
4 The notice says that the shop is open every day from 8.30. It is 9 o'clock now, but the shop isn't open yet.
_____
5 The speed limit is 30 miles an hour, but Kate is doing 50.
She _____
6 Laura gave me her address, but I didn't write it down. Now I can't remember it.
I _____
7 I was driving behind another car. Suddenly, the driver in front stopped without warning and I drove into the back of his car. It wasn't my fault.
The driver in front _____
8 I walked into a wall. I was looking behind me. I wasn't looking where I was going.
_____

Unit 34 - Should 2 - lesson

You can use **should** after a number of verbs, especially:

    demand   insist   propose   recommend   suggest

- They **insisted** that we **should have** dinner with them.
- I **demanded** that he **should apologise**.
- What do you **suggest I should do?**
- I **insist** that something **should be done** about the problem.

We also say '**It's important/vital/necessary/essential** that ... **should** ...':
- It's **essential** that everyone **should be** here on time.

You can also leave out **should** in all the sentences in Section A:
- It's **essential** that everyone **be** here on time.   (= that everyone **should be** here)
- I **demanded** that he **apologise**. (= that he **should apologise**)
- What do you **suggest I do?**
- I **insist** that something **be done** about the problem.

This form (**be/do/have/apologise** etc.) is sometimes called the *subjunctive*. It is the same as the *infinitive* (without **to**).
You can also use normal present and past tenses:
- It's **essential** that everyone **is** here on time.
- I **demanded** that he **apologised**.

After **suggest**, you cannot use **to** ... ('to do / to buy' etc.). You can say:
- What do you **suggest we should do?**
or   What do you **suggest we do?** (*but not* What do you suggest us to do?)
- Jane **suggested** that I (**should**) **buy** a car.
or   Jane **suggested** that I **bought** a car. (*but not* Jane suggested me to buy)

You can also use -ing after **suggest**: What do you **suggest doing?** See Unit 53.

You can use **should** after a number of adjectives, especially:

    strange   odd   funny   typical   natural   interesting   surprised   surprising

- It's **strange** that he **should be** late. He's usually on time.
- I was **surprised** that he **should say** such a thing.

If ... should ...

You can say '**If** something **should** happen ...' . For example:
- **If** Tom **should phone** while I'm out, tell him I'll call him back later.

'**If** Tom **should phone**' is similar to '**If** Tom **phones**'. With **should**, the speaker feels that the possibility is smaller. Another example:
- We have no jobs at present. But **if** the situation **should change**, we'll let you know.

You can also begin these sentences with **should** (**Should** something happen ...):
- **Should** Tom **phone**, tell him I'll call him back later.

You can use **I should** ... / **I shouldn't** ... to give somebody advice. For example:
- 'Shall I leave now?'   'No, **I should** wait a bit longer.'
Here, **I should wait** = I would wait if I were you, I advise you to wait.
Two more examples:
- 'I'm going out now. Is it cold?'   'Yes, **I should wear** a coat.
- **I shouldn't stay** up too late. You'll be tired tomorrow.

Unit 34 - Should 2 - exercises

34.1 Write a sentence (beginning in the way shown) that means the same as the first sentence.

1 'I think it would be a good idea to see a specialist,' the doctor said to me.
The doctor recommended that ___I should see a specialist___ .

2 'You really must stay a little longer,' she said to me.
She insisted that I _____ .

3 'Why don't you visit the museum after lunch?' I said to them.
I suggested that _____ .

4 'You must pay the rent by Friday,' the landlord said to us.
The landlord demanded that _____ .

5 'Why don't you go away for a few days?' Jack said to me.
Jack suggested that _____ .

34.2 Are these sentences right or wrong?

1 a Tom suggested that I should look for another job. ___OK___
  b Tom suggested that I look for another job. ___OK___
  c Tom suggested that I looked for another job. ___OK___
  d Tom suggested me to look for another job. ___NO___

2 a Where do you suggest I go for my holiday? ___OK___
  b Where do you suggest me to go for my holiday? ___NO___
  c Where do you suggest I should go for my holiday? ___OK___

34.3 Complete the sentences using should + the following:

   ask   ~~be~~   leave   listen   say   worry

1 It's strange that he ___should be___ late. He's usually on time.
2 It's funny that you _____ that. I was going to say the same thing.
3 It's only natural that parents _____ about their children.
4 Isn't it typical of Joe that he _____ without saying goodbye to anybody?
5 I was surprised that they _____ me for advice. What advice could I give them?
6 I'm going to give you all some essential information, so it's important that everybody
_____ very carefully.

34.4 Use the words in brackets to complete these sentences. Use If ... should ... .

1 I'm going out now. ___If Tom should phone___ , tell him I'll call him back this evening.
(Tom / phone)

2 I've hung the washing out to dry on the balcony. _____ ,
can you bring the washing in, please? (it / rain)

3 I think everything will be OK. _____ any problems,
I'm sure we'll be able to solve them. (there / be)

4 I don't want anyone to know where I'm going. _____ ,
just say that you don't know. (anyone / ask)

Write sentences 3 and 4 again, this time beginning with Should.

5 (3) Should _____ , I'm sure we'll be able to solve them.
6 (4) _____ , just say that you don't know.

34.5 (Section E) Complete the sentences using I should + the following:

   buy   keep   phone   ~~wait~~

1 'Shall I leave now?' 'No, ___I should wait___ a bit longer.'
2 'Shall I throw these things away?' 'No, _____ them. You may need them.'
3 'Shall I go and see Paul?' 'Yes, but _____ him first.'
4 'Is it worth repairing this TV set?' 'No, _____ a new one.'

Unit 35 - Had better/It's time… -   lesson

Had better (I'd better / you'd better etc.)

I'd better do something = it is advisable to do it. If I don't do it, there will be a problem or a danger:
- □ I have to meet Ann in ten minutes. **I'd better go** now or I'll be late.
- □ 'Shall I take an umbrella?'   'Yes, **you'd better**. It might rain.'
- □ **We'd better stop** for petrol soon. The tank is almost empty.

The negative is **I'd better not** (= I **had** better not):
- □ 'Are you going out tonight?'   '**I'd better not**. I've got a lot to do.'
- □ You don't look very well. **You'd better not go** to work today.

Remember that:

The form is '**had better**' (usually '**I'd better / you'd better**' etc. in spoken English).
- □ **I'd better** phone Carol, hadn't I?

Had is normally past, but the meaning of **had better** is present or future, *not* past.
- □ **I'd better go** to the bank **now / tomorrow**.

We say '**I'd better do**' (*not* to do).
- □ It might rain. We'd better **take** an umbrella. (*not* We'd better to take)

Had better and should

Had better is similar to **should** but not exactly the same. We use **had better** only for a specific situation (not for things in general). You can use **should** in all types of situations to give an opinion or give advice:
- □ It's late. **You'd better go**. / You **should go**. (a specific situation)
- □ You're always at home. You **should go** out more often. (in general – *not* 'had better go')

Also, with **had better**, there is always a danger or a problem if you don't follow the advice. **Should** only means 'it is a good thing to do'. Compare:
- □ It's a great film. You **should** go and see it. (but no problem if you don't)
- □ The film starts at 8.30. You'**d better** go now or you'll be late.

It's time …

You can say **It's time** (for somebody) **to** … :
- □ It's time **to go** home. / It's time for us **to go** home.

But you can also say:
- □ It's late. It's time **we went** home.
Here we use the past (**went**), but the meaning is present, *not* past:
- □ It's 10 o'clock and he's still in bed. **It's time** he **got** up. (*not* It's time he gets up)

It's time you did something = you should have already done it or started it. We often use this structure to criticise or to complain:
- □ **It's time** the children **were** in bed. It's long after their bedtime.
- □ You're very selfish. **It's time** you **realised** that you're not the most important person in the world.

You can also say **It's about time** … . This makes the criticism stronger:
- □ Jack is a great talker. But **it's about time** he **did** something instead of just talking.

Unit 35 - Had better/It's time... - exercises

35.1 Read the situations and write sentences with **had better** or **had better not**. Use the words in brackets.

1 You're going out for a walk with Tom. It looks as if it might rain. You say to Tom:
(an umbrella) _We'd better take an umbrella._

2 Michael has just cut himself. It's a bad cut. You say to him:
(a plaster) _____

3 You and Kate plan to go to a restaurant this evening. It's a popular restaurant. You say to Kate:
(reserve) We _____

4 Jill doesn't look very well – not well enough to go to work. You say to her:
(work) _____

5 You received the phone bill four weeks ago, but you haven't paid it yet. If you don't pay soon, you could be in trouble. You say to yourself:
(pay) _____

6 You want to go out, but you're expecting an important phone call. You say to your friend:
(go out) I _____

7 You and Liz are going to the theatre. You've missed the bus and you don't want to be late.
You say to Liz: (a taxi) _____

35.2 Put in **had better** where suitable. If **had better** is not suitable, use **should**.

1 I have an appointment in ten minutes. I _'d better_ go now or I'll be late.
2 It's a great film. You _should_ go and see it. You'll really like it.
3 I _____ get up early tomorrow. I've got a lot to do.
4 When people are driving, they _____ keep their eyes on the road.
5 I'm glad you came to see us. You _____ come more often.
6 She'll be upset if we don't invite her to the wedding, so we _____ invite her.
7 These biscuits are delicious. You _____ try one.
8 I think everybody _____ learn a foreign language.

35.3 Complete the sentences. Sometimes you need only one word, sometimes two.

1 a I need some money. I'd better _go_ to the bank.
  b John is expecting you to phone him. You _____ better phone him now.
  c 'Shall I leave the window open?' 'No, you'd better _____ it.'
  d We'd better leave as soon as possible, _____ we?
2 a It's time the government _____ something about the problem.
  b It's time something _____ about the problem.
  c I think it's about time you _____ about other people instead of only thinking about yourself.

35.4 Read the situations and write sentences with **It's time (somebody did** something).

1 You think the children should be in bed. It's already 11 o'clock.
  It's time the children were in bed.

2 You haven't had a holiday for a very long time. You need one now.
  It's time I _____

3 You're sitting on a train waiting for it to leave the station. It's already five minutes late.
  _____

4 You enjoy having parties. You haven't had one for a long time.
  _____

5 The company you work for has been badly managed for a long time. You think some changes should be made.
  _____

6 Andrew has been doing the same job for the last ten years. He should try something else.
  _____

Unit 36 - Would - lesson

We use **would** (**'d**) / **wouldn't** when we *imagine* a situation or action (= we think of something that is not real):

- It **would be** nice to buy a new car, but we can't afford it.
- I'**d love** to live by the sea.
- A: Shall I tell Chris what happened?
  B: No, I **wouldn't say** anything.
  (= I wouldn't say anything in your situation)

We use **would have** (**done**) when we imagine situations or actions in the past (= things that didn't happen):

- They helped us a lot. I don't know what we'**d have done** (= we **would have done**) without their help.
- I didn't tell Sam what happened. He **wouldn't have been** pleased.

Compare **would** (**do**) and **would have** (**done**):

- I **would phone** Sue, but I haven't got her number. *(now)*
  I **would have phoned** Sue, but I didn't have her number. *(past)*
- I'm not going to invite them to the party. They **wouldn't come** anyway.
  I didn't invite them to the party. They **wouldn't have come** anyway.

We often use **would** in sentences with **if** (see Units 38–40):

- I **would phone** Sue if I had her number.
- I **would have phoned** Sue if I'd had her number.

Compare **will** (**'ll**) and **would** (**'d**):

- I'**ll stay** a bit longer. I've got plenty of time.
  I'**d stay** a bit longer, but I really have to go now. (so I can't stay longer)
- I'**ll phone** Sue. I've got her number.
  I'**d phone** Sue, but I haven't got her number. (so I can't phone her)

Sometimes **would**/**wouldn't** is the past of **will**/**won't**. Compare:

present		*past*
TOM: I'**ll phone** you on Sunday.	→	Tom said he'**d phone** me on Sunday.
ANN: I promise I **won't be** late.	→	Ann promised that she **wouldn't be** late.
LIZ: Damn! The car **won't start.**	→	Liz was annoyed because her car **wouldn't start.**

Somebody **wouldn't do** something = he/she refused to do it:

- I tried to warn him, but he **wouldn't listen** to me. (= he refused to listen)
- The car **wouldn't start.** (= it 'refused' to start)

You can also use **would** when you talk about things that happened regularly in the past:

- When we were children, we lived by the sea. In summer, if the weather was fine, we **would** all get up early and go for a swim. (= we did this regularly)
- Whenever Richard was angry, he **would** walk out of the room.

With this meaning, **would** is similar to **used to** (see Unit 18):

- Whenever Richard was angry, he **used to walk** out of the room.

Unit 36 - Would - exercises

36.1 Write sentences about yourself. Imagine things you would like or wouldn't like.

1 (a place you'd love to live) __I'd love to live by the sea.__
2 (a job you wouldn't like to do) _____
3 (something you would love to do) _____
4 (something that would be nice to have) _____
5 (a place you'd like to go to) _____

36.2 Complete the sentences using **would** + the following verbs (in the correct form):

be   be   ~~do~~   do   enjoy   enjoy   have   pass   stop

1 They helped us a lot. I don't know what we __would have done__ without their help.
2 You should go and see the film. You _____ it.
3 It's a pity you couldn't come to the concert yesterday. You _____ it.
4 Shall I apply for the job or not? What _____ you _____ in my position?
5 I was in a hurry when I saw you. Otherwise I _____ to talk.
6 We took a taxi home last night but got stuck in the traffic. It _____ quicker to walk.
7 Why don't you go and see Clare? She _____ very pleased to see you.
8 Why didn't you do the exam? I'm sure you _____ it.
9 In an ideal world, everybody _____ enough to eat.

36.3 Each sentence on the right follows a sentence on the left. Which follows which?

1 ~~I'd like to go to Australia one day.~~	a It wouldn't have been very nice.	1c
2 I wouldn't like to live on a busy road.	b It would have been fun.	....
3 I'm sorry the trip was cancelled.	c ~~It would be nice.~~	....
4 I'm looking forward to going out tonight.	d It won't be much fun.	....
5 I'm glad we didn't go out in the rain.	e It wouldn't be very nice.	....
6 I'm not looking forward to the trip.	f It will be fun.	....

36.4 Write sentences using **promised** + **would/wouldn't**.

1 I wonder why Laura is late. __She promised she wouldn't be late.__
2 I wonder why Steve hasn't phoned. He promised _____
3 Why did you tell Jane what I said? You _____
4 I'm surprised they didn't wait for us. They _____

36.5 Complete the sentences. Use **wouldn't** + a suitable verb.

1 I tried to warn him, but he __wouldn't listen__ to me.
2 I asked Amanda what had happened, but she _____ me.
3 Paul was very angry about what I'd said and _____ to me for two weeks.
4 Martina insisted on carrying all her luggage. She _____ me help her.

36.6 These sentences are about things that often happened in the past. Complete the sentences using **would** + the following: forget   help   shake   share   ~~walk~~

1 Whenever Richard was angry, he __would walk__ out of the room.
2 We used to live next to a railway line. Every time a train went past, the house _____ .
3 George was a very kind man. He _____ always _____ you if you had a problem.
4 Brenda was always very generous. She didn't have much, but she _____ what she had with everyone else.
5 You could never rely on Joe. It didn't matter how many times you reminded him to do something, he _____ always _____ .

Unit 37 - Can/Could/Would you... ? - lesson

Asking people to do things (requests)

We use **can** or **could** to ask people to do things:
- □ **Can you** wait a moment, please?
- *or* **Could you** wait a moment, please?
- □ Liz, **can you** do me a favour?
- □ Excuse me, **could you** tell me how to get to the airport?

Note that we say **Do you think** you could ... ? (*not* can):
- □ **Do you think you could** lend me some money until next week?

We also use **will** and **would** to ask people to do things (but **can/could** are more usual):
- □ Liz, **will you** do me a favour?
- □ **Would you** please be quiet? I'm trying to concentrate.

> Could you open the door, please?

Asking for things

To ask for something, we use **Can I have** ... ? or **Could I have** ... ?:
- □ *(in a shop)* **Can I have** these postcards, please?
- □ *(during a meal)* **Could I have** the salt, please?

May I have ... ? is also possible:
- □ **May I have** these postcards, please?

Asking to do things

To ask to do something, we use **can, could** or **may**:
- □ *(on the phone)* Hello, **can I** speak to Steve, please?
- □ '**Could I** use your phone?' 'Yes, of course.'
- □ **Do you think I could** borrow your bike?
- □ '**May I** come in?' 'Yes, please do.'

May is more formal than **can** or **could**.

To ask to do something, you can also say **Do you mind if I** ... ? or **Is it all right / Is it OK if I** ... ?:
- □ '**Do you mind if I** use your phone?' 'Sure. Go ahead.'
- □ '**Is it all right if I** come in?' 'Yes, of course.'

Offering to do things

To offer to do something, you can use **Can I** ... ?:
- □ '**Can I** get you a cup of coffee?' 'That would be nice.'
- □ '**Can I** help you?' 'No, it's all right. I can manage.'

Offering and inviting

To offer or to invite, we use **Would you like** ... ? (*not* Do you like):
- □ '**Would you like** a cup of coffee?' 'Yes, please.'
- □ '**Would you like** to come to dinner tomorrow evening?' 'I'd love to.'

I'd like ... is a polite way of saying what you want:
- □ *(at a tourist information office)* **I'd like** some information about hotels, please.
- □ *(in a shop)* **I'd like** to try on this jacket, please.

Unit 37 - Can/Could/Would you... ? - exercises

37.1 Read the situations and write questions beginning Can ... or Could ... .

1 You're carrying a lot of things. You can't open the door yourself. There's a man standing near the door. You say to him: _Could you open the door, please?_

2 You phone Sue, but somebody else answers. Sue isn't there. You want to leave a message for her. You say: _____

3 You're a tourist. You want to go to the station, but you don't know how to get there. You ask at your hotel: _____

4 You are in a clothes shop. You see some trousers you like and you want to try them on. You say to the shop assistant: _____

5 You have a car. You have to go the same way as Steve, who is on foot. You offer him a lift. You say to him: _____

37.2 Read the situation and write a question using the word in brackets.

1 You want to borrow your friend's camera. What do you say to him?
(think) _Do you think I could borrow your camera?_

2 You are at a friend's house and you want to use her phone. What do you say?
(all right) _Is it all right if I use your phone?_

3 You've written a letter in English. Before you send it, you want a friend to check it for you. What do you ask?
(think) _____

4 You want to leave work early. What do you ask your boss?
(mind) _____

5 The woman in the next room is playing music. It's very loud. You want her to turn it down. What do you say to her?
(think) _____

6 You're on a train. The window is open and you're feeling cold. You'd like to close it, but first you ask the woman next to you.
(OK) _____

7 You're still on the train. The woman next to you has finished reading her newspaper, and you'd like to have a look at it. You ask her.
(think) _____

37.3 What would you say in these situations?

1 Paul has come to see you in your flat. You offer him something to eat.
YOU: _Would you like something to eat_   ?
PAUL: No, thank you. I've just eaten.

2 You need help to change the film in your camera. You ask Kate.
YOU: I don't know how to change the film. _____ ?
KATE: Sure. It's easy. All you have to do is this.

3 You're on a bus. You have a seat, but an elderly man is standing. You offer him your seat.
YOU: _____ ?
MAN: Oh, that's very kind of you. Thank you very much.

4 You're the passenger in a car. Your friend is driving very fast. You ask her to slow down.
YOU: You're making me very nervous. _____ ?
DRIVER: Oh, I'm sorry. I didn't realise I was going so fast.

5 You've finished your meal in a restaurant and now you want the bill. You ask the waiter:
YOU: _____ ?
WAITER: Right. I'll get it for you now.

6 A friend of yours is interested in one of your books. You invite him to borrow it.
FRIEND: This looks very interesting.
YOU: Yes, it's a good book. _____ ?

Unit 38 - If I do... and If I did... - lesson

Compare these examples:

(1) Lisa has lost her watch. She tells Sue:

LISA: I've lost my watch. Have you seen it anywhere?
SUE: No, but **if I find** it, I'll tell you.

In this example, Sue feels there is a real possibility that she will find the watch. So she says:
if I find ... , I'll ... .

(2) Joe says:

If **I found** a wallet in the street, I'd take it to the police station.

This is a different type of situation. Here, Joe doesn't expect to find a wallet in the street; he is *imagining* a situation that will probably not happen. So he says:
if I found ... , I'd (= I would) ... . (*not* if I find ... , I'll ...)

When you imagine something like this, you use if + *past*
(**if I found** / **if there was** / **if we didn't** etc.).
But the meaning is *not* past:

□ What would you do **if you won** a million pounds?
(we don't really expect this to happen)
□ I don't really want to go to their party, but I
probably will go. They'd be upset **if I didn't** go.
□ **If there was** (*or* were) an election tomorrow,
who would you vote for?

For if ... was/were, see Unit 39C.

(If I won a million pounds ...)

We do not normally use **would** in the **if**-part of the sentence:

□ I'd be very frightened **if somebody pointed** a gun at me. (*not* if somebody would point)
□ **If I didn't** go to their party, they'd be upset. (*not* If I wouldn't go)

But you can use **if** ... **would** when you ask somebody to do something:

□ *(from a formal letter)* I would be grateful **if you would let** me know your decision as soon
as possible.

In the other part of the sentence (not the if-part) we use **would** ('**d**) / **wouldn't**:

□ If you took more exercise, you'**d** (= you would) feel better.
□ I'm not tired. If I went to bed now, I **wouldn't sleep**.
□ **Would** you **mind** if I used your phone?

Could and **might** are also possible:

□ If you took more exercise, you **might feel** better. (= it is possible that you would feel better)
□ If it stopped raining, we **could go** out. (= we would be able to go out)

Do not use **when** in sentences like those on this page:

□ They'd be upset **if I didn't** go to their party. (*not* when I didn't go)
□ What would you do **if you were** bitten by a snake? (*not* when you were bitten)

Unit 38 - If I do... and If I did... - exercises

38.1 Put the verb into the correct form.

1 They would be offended if I ___didn't go___ to their party. (not / go)
2 If you took more exercise, you ___would feel___ better. (feel)
3 If they offered me the job, I think I _____ it. (take)
4 A lot of people would be out of work if the car factory _____ . (close down)
5 If I sold my car, I _____ much money for it. (not / get)
6 (in a lift) What would happen if somebody _____ that red button? (press)
7 I don't think there's any chance that Gary and Emma will get married. I'd be absolutely astonished if they _____ . (do)
8 Liz gave me this ring. She _____ very upset if I lost it. (be)
9 Dave and Kate are expecting us. They would be very disappointed if we _____ . (not / come)
10 Would Steve mind if I _____ his bike without asking him? (borrow)
11 What would you do if somebody _____ in here with a gun? (walk)
12 I'm sure Sue _____ if you explained the situation to her. (understand)

38.2 You ask a friend to imagine these situations. You ask What would you do if ... ?

1 (imagine – you win a lot of money)
___What would you do if you won a lot of money?___
2 (imagine – you lose your passport)
What _____
3 (imagine – there's a fire in the building)
_____
4 (imagine – you're in a lift and it stops between floors)
_____

38.3 Answer the questions in the way shown.

1 A: Shall we catch the 10.30 train?
  B: No. (arrive too early) ___If we caught the 10.30 train, we'd arrive too early.___
2 A: Is Kevin going to take his driving test?
  B: No. (fail) If he _____
3 A: Why don't we stay at a hotel?
  B: No. (cost too much) If _____
4 A: Is Sally going to apply for the job?
  B: No. (not / get it) If _____
5 A: Let's tell them the truth.
  B: No. (not / believe us) If _____
6 A: Why don't we invite Bill to the party?
  B: No. (have to invite his friends too) _____

38.4 Use your own ideas to complete these sentences.

1 If you took more exercise, ___you'd feel better.___
2 I'd be very angry if _____
3 If I didn't go to work tomorrow, _____
4 Would you go to the party if _____
5 If you bought some new clothes, _____
6 Would you mind if _____

Unit 39 - If I knew... I wish I knew - lesson

Study this example situation:

Sarah wants to phone Paul, but she can't do this because she doesn't know his number.
She says:

If I knew his number, I **would phone** him.

Sarah says: **If I knew** his number ... . This tells us that she *doesn't* know his number. She is imagining the situation. The *real* situation is that she doesn't know his number.

If I knew his number ...

When you imagine a situation like this, you use **if** + *past* (if I knew / if you were / if we didn't etc.). But the meaning is present, *not* past:
- □ Tom would read more if he **had** more time. (but he doesn't have much time)
- □ **If I didn't** want to go to the party, I wouldn't go. (but I want to go)
- □ We wouldn't have any money **if we didn't** work. (but we work)
- □ **If you were** in my position, what would you do?
- □ It's a pity you can't drive. It would be useful **if you could**.

We use the past in the same way after **wish** (I wish I **knew** / I wish you **were** etc.). We use **wish** to say that we regret something, that something is not as we would like it to be:
- □ I **wish** I **knew** Paul's phone number.
  (= I don't know it and I regret this)
- □ Do you ever **wish** you **could** fly?
  (you can't fly)
- □ It rains a lot here. I **wish** it **didn't** rain so often.
- □ It's very crowded here. I **wish** there **weren't** so many people. (there are a lot of people)
- □ I **wish** I **didn't** have to work tomorrow, but unfortunately I do.

I wish I had an umbrella.

If I were / if I was

After **if** and **wish**, you can use **were** instead of **was** (if I were ... / I wish it were etc.). I **was** / it **was** are also possible. So you can say:
- □ If I **were** you, I wouldn't buy that coat.   *or*   If I **was** you, ...
- □ I'd go out **if it weren't** so cold.   *or*   ... **if it wasn't** so cold.
- □ I wish Carol **were** here.   *or*   I wish Carol **was** here.

We do not normally use **would** in the **if**-part of the sentence or after **wish**:
- □ If I **were** rich, I **would** have a yacht. (*not* If I would be rich)
- □ I **wish** I **had** something to read. (*not* I wish I would have)

Sometimes **wish ... would** is possible: I **wish you would listen**. See Unit 41.

Could sometimes means 'would be able to' and sometimes 'was/were able to':
- □ You **could** get a better job   (you **could** get = you would be able to get)
  if you **could** use a computer.   (you **could** use = you were able to use)

Unit 39 - If I knew... I wish I knew - exercises

39.1 **Put the verb into the correct form.**

1 If I __knew__ (know) his number, I would phone him.
2 I __wouldn't buy__ (not / buy) that coat if I were you.
3 I .... (help) you if I could, but I'm afraid I can't.
4 We would need a car if we .... (live) in the country.
5 If we had the choice, we .... (live) in the country.
6 This soup isn't very good. It .... (taste) better if it wasn't so salty.
7 I wouldn't mind living in England if the weather .... (be) better.
8 If I were you, I .... (not / wait). I .... (go) now.
9 You're always tired. If you .... (not / go) to bed so late every night, you wouldn't be tired all the time.
10 I think there are too many cars. If there .... (not / be) so many cars, there .... (not / be) so much pollution.

39.2 **Write a sentence with if ... for each situation.**

1 We don't see you very often because you live so far away.
   __If you didn't live so far away, we'd see you more often.__
2 This book is too expensive, so I'm not going to buy it.
   I'd .... if ....
3 We don't go out very often – we can't afford it.
   We ....
4 I can't meet you tomorrow – I have to work late.
   If ....
5 It's raining, so we can't have lunch outside.
   We ....
6 I don't want his advice, and that's why I'm not going to ask for it.
   If ....

39.3 **Write sentences beginning I wish ... .**

1 I don't know many people (and I'm lonely). __I wish I knew more people.__
2 I don't have a mobile phone (and I need one). I wish ....
3 Helen isn't here (and I need to see her). ....
4 It's cold (and I hate cold weather). ....
5 I live in a big city (and I don't like it). ....
6 I can't go to the party (and I'd like to). ....
7 I have to work tomorrow (but I'd like to stay in bed).
   ....
8 I don't know anything about cars (and my car has just broken down).
   ....
9 I'm not feeling well (and it's not nice).
   ....

39.4 **Write your own sentences beginning I wish ... .**

1 (somewhere you'd like to be now – on the beach, in New York, in bed etc.)
   I wish I ....
2 (something you'd like to have – a computer, a job, lots of money etc.)
   ....
3 (something you'd like to be able to do – sing, speak a language, fly etc.)
   ....
4 (something you'd like to be – beautiful, strong, rich etc.)
   ....

Unit 40 - If I had known... I wish I had known - lesson

Study this example situation:

Last month Gary was in hospital for a few days. Rachel didn't know this, so she didn't go to visit him. They met a few days ago. Rachel said:

If I had known you were in hospital, **I would have gone** to see you.

Rachel said: **If I had known** you were in hospital ... . This tells us that she *didn't* know he was in hospital.

We use **if + had** (**'d**) ... to talk about the past (**if I had known/been/done** etc.):
  - □ I didn't see you when you passed me in the street. **If I'd seen** you, of course I would have said hello. (but I didn't see you)
  - □ I decided to stay at home last night. I would have gone out **if I hadn't been** so tired. (but I was tired)
  - □ **If he had been looking** where he was going, he wouldn't have walked into the wall. (but he wasn't looking)
  - □ The view was wonderful. **If I'd had** a camera with me, I would have taken some photographs. (but I didn't have a camera)

Compare:
  - □ I'm not hungry. **If I was** hungry, I would eat something. *(now)*
  - □ I wasn't hungry. **If I had been** hungry, I would have eaten something. *(past)*

Do not use **would** in the if-part of the sentence. We use **would** in the other part of the sentence:
  - □ **If I had seen** you, **I would have said** hello. (*not* If I would have seen you)

Note that **'d** can be **would** or **had**:
  - □ If **I'd seen** you,   (I'd seen = I had seen)
    I'd have said hello. (I'd have said = I **would** have said)

We use **had** (**done**) in the same way after **wish**. **I wish** something **had happened** = I am sorry that it didn't happen:
  - □ **I wish I'd known** that Gary was ill. I would have gone to see him. (but I didn't know)
  - □ I feel sick. **I wish I hadn't eaten** so much cake. (I ate too much cake)
  - □ Do you **wish** you **had studied** science instead of languages? (you didn't study science)

Do not use **would have** ... after **wish**:
  - □ The weather was cold while we were away. I wish it **had been** warmer. (*not* I wish it would have been)

Compare **would** (**do**) and **would have** (**done**):
  - □ If I had gone to the party last night, **I would be** tired now. (I am not tired now – *present*)
  - □ If I had gone to the party last night, **I would have met** lots of people. (I didn't meet lots of people – *past*)

Compare **would have**, **could have** and **might have**:

□ If the weather hadn't been so bad, {
  we **would have gone** out.
  we **could have gone** out.
    (= we would have been able to go out)
  we **might have gone** out.
    (= perhaps we would have gone out)
}

Unit 40 - If I had known... I wish I had known - exercises

40.1 Put the verb into the correct form.

1 I didn't know you were in hospital. If _I'd known_ (I / know), _I would have gone_ (I / go) to see you.

2 Sam got to the station just in time to catch the train to the airport. If _____ (he / miss) the train, _____ (he / miss) his flight.

3 I'm glad that you reminded me about Amanda's birthday. _____ (I / forget) if _____ (you / not / remind) me.

4 Unfortunately I forgot my address book when I went on holiday. If _____ (I / have) your address, _____ (I / send) you a postcard.

5 A: How was your holiday? Did you have a nice time?
   B: It was OK, but _____ (we / enjoy) it more if _____ (the weather / be) nicer.

6 I took a taxi to the hotel, but the traffic was bad. _____ (it / be) quicker if _____ (I / walk).

7 I'm not tired. If _____ (I / be) tired, I'd go home now.

8 I wasn't tired last night. If _____ (I / be) tired, I would have gone home earlier.

40.2 For each situation, write a sentence beginning with If.

1 I wasn't hungry, so I didn't eat anything.
   If I'd been hungry, I would have eaten something.

2 The accident happened because the road was icy.
   If the road _____

3 I didn't know that Joe had to get up early, so I didn't wake him up.
   If I _____

4 I was able to buy the car only because Jane lent me the money.
   _____

5 Karen wasn't injured in the crash because she was wearing a seat belt.
   _____

6 You didn't have any breakfast – that's why you're hungry now.
   _____

7 I didn't get a taxi because I didn't have any money.
   _____

40.3 Imagine that you are in these situations. For each situation, write a sentence with I wish.

1 You've eaten too much and now you feel sick.
   You say: _I wish I hadn't eaten so much._

2 There was a job advertised in the newspaper. You decided not to apply for it. Now you think that your decision was wrong.
   You say: I wish I _____

3 When you were younger, you never learned to play a musical instrument. Now you regret this.
   You say: _____

4 You've painted the gate red. Now you think that red was the wrong colour.
   You say: _____

5 You are walking in the country. You'd like to take some photographs, but you didn't bring your camera.
   You say: _____

6 You have some unexpected guests. They didn't phone first to say they were coming. You are very busy and you are not prepared for them.
   You say (to yourself): _____

85

Unit 41 - Wish - lesson

You can say 'I wish you luck / every success / a happy birthday' etc. :
- □ I wish you every success in the future.
- □ I saw Tim before the exam and he wished me luck.

We say 'wish somebody *something*' (luck / a happy birthday etc.). But you cannot 'wish that something *happens*'. We use hope in this situation. For example:
- □ I hope you get this letter before you go away. (*not* I wish you get)

Compare I wish and I hope:
- □ I wish you a pleasant stay here.
- □ I hope you have a pleasant stay here. (*not* I wish you have)

We also use wish to say that we regret something, that something is not as we would like it. When we use wish in this way, we use the *past* (knew/lived etc.), but the meaning is *present*:
- □ I wish I knew what to do about the problem. (I don't know and I regret this)
- □ I wish you didn't have to go so soon. (you have to go)
- □ Do you wish you lived near the sea? (you don't live near the sea)
- □ Jack's going on a trip to Mexico soon. I wish I was going too. (I'm not going)

To say that we regret something in the past, we use wish + had ... (had known / had said) etc. :
- □ I wish I'd known about the party. I would have gone if I'd known. (I didn't know)
- □ It was a stupid thing to say. I wish I hadn't said it. (I said it)

For more examples, see Units 39 and 40.

I wish I could (do something) = I regret that I cannot do it:
- □ I'm sorry I have to go. I wish I could stay longer. (but I can't)
- □ I've met that man before. I wish I could remember his name. (but I can't)

I wish I could have (done something) = I regret that I could not do it:
- □ I hear the party was great. I wish I could have gone. (but I couldn't go)

You can say 'I wish (somebody) would (do something)'. For example:

I wish it would stop raining.

It's been raining all day. Jill doesn't like it. She says:
I wish it would stop raining.

Jill would like the rain to stop, but this will probably not happen.

We use I wish ... would when we would like something to happen or change. Usually, the speaker doesn't expect this to happen.

We often use I wish ... would to complain about a situation:
- □ The phone has been ringing for five minutes. I wish somebody would answer it.
- □ I wish you would do something instead of just sitting and doing nothing.

You can use I wish ... wouldn't ... to complain about things that people do repeatedly:
- □ I wish you wouldn't keep interrupting me.

We use I wish ... would ... for actions and changes, *not* situations. Compare:
- □ I wish Sarah would come. (= I want her to come)

but   I wish Sarah was (*or* were) here now. (*not* I wish Sarah would be)

- □ I wish somebody would buy me a car.

but   I wish I had a car. (*not* I wish I would have)

Unit 41 - Wish - exercises

41.1 Put in **wish(ed)** or **hope(d)**.

1 I .....wish..... you a pleasant stay here.
2 Enjoy your holiday. I .... you have a great time.
3 Goodbye. I .... you all the best.
4 We said goodbye to each other and .... each other luck.
5 We're going to have a picnic tomorrow, so I .... the weather is nice.
6 I .... you luck in your new job. I .... it works out well for you.

41.2 What do you say in these situations? Write sentences with **I wish ... would ...** .

1 It's raining. You want to go out, but not in the rain.
You say: .....I wish it would stop raining.....
2 You're waiting for Jane. She's late and you're getting impatient.
You say to yourself: I wish ....
3 You're looking for a job – so far without success. Nobody will give you a job.
You say: I wish somebody ....
4 You can hear a baby crying. It's been crying for a long time and you're trying to study.
You say: ....
5 Brian has been wearing the same clothes for years. You think he needs some new clothes.
You say to Brian: ....

For the following situations, write sentences with **I wish ... wouldn't ...** .

6 Your friend drives very fast. You don't like this.
You say to your friend: I wish you ....
7 Joe leaves the door open all the time. This annoys you.
You say to Joe: ....
8 A lot of people drop litter in the street. You don't like this.
You say: I wish people ....

41.3 Are these sentences right or wrong? Correct them where necessary.

1 I wish Sarah would be here now.　　　.....I wish Sarah were here now.....
2 I wish you would listen to me.　　　...........................
3 I wish I would have more free time.　　　...........................
4 I wish our flat would be a bit bigger.　　　...........................
5 I wish the weather would change.　　　...........................
6 I wish you wouldn't complain all the time.　　　...........................
7 I wish everything wouldn't be so expensive.　　　...........................

41.4 Put the verb into the correct form.

1 It was a stupid thing to say. I wish I .....hadn't said..... it. (I / not / say)
2 I'm fed up with this rain. I wish .....it would stop..... . (it / stop)
3 It's a difficult question. I wish .... the answer. (I / know)
4 I should have listened to you. I wish .... your advice. (I / take)
5 You're lucky to be going away. I wish .... with you. (I / can / come)
6 I have no energy at the moment. I wish .... so tired. (I / not / be)
7 Aren't they ready yet? I wish .... up. (they / hurry)
8 It would be nice to stay here longer. I wish .... to leave now.
(we / not / have)
9 When we were in London last year, we didn't have time to see all the things we wanted to see.
I wish .... longer. (we / can / stay)
10 It's freezing today. I wish .... so cold. I hate cold weather. (it / not / be)
11 Joe still doesn't know what he wants to do. I wish .... (he / decide)
12 I really didn't enjoy the party. I wish .... (we / not / go)

Unit 42 - Passive 1 - lesson

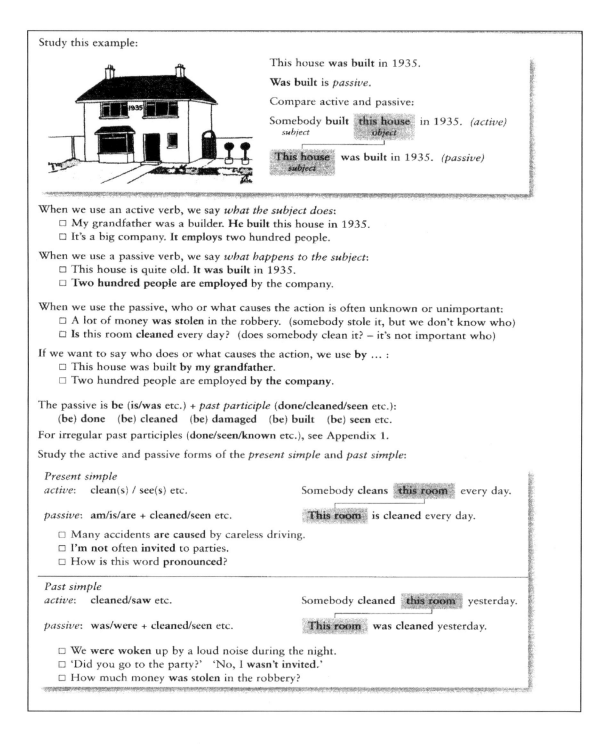

Study this example:

This house **was built** in 1935.

Was built is *passive*.

Compare active and passive:

Somebody **built** this house in 1935. *(active)*
subject   object

This house was built in 1935. *(passive)*
subject

When we use an active verb, we say *what the subject does*:
- ☐ My grandfather was a builder. **He built** this house in 1935.
- ☐ It's a big company. It **employs** two hundred people.

When we use a passive verb, we say *what happens to the subject*:
- ☐ This house is quite old. **It was built** in 1935.
- ☐ **Two hundred people are employed** by the company.

When we use the passive, who or what causes the action is often unknown or unimportant:
- ☐ A lot of money **was stolen** in the robbery. (somebody stole it, but we don't know who)
- ☐ **Is** this room **cleaned** every day? (does somebody clean it? – it's not important who)

If we want to say who does or what causes the action, we use **by** ... :
- ☐ This house was built **by my grandfather**.
- ☐ Two hundred people are employed **by the company**.

The passive is **be** (**is/was** etc.) + *past participle* (**done/cleaned/seen** etc.):
   (be) done   (be) cleaned   (be) damaged   (be) built   (be) seen etc.

For irregular past participles (**done/seen/known** etc.), see Appendix 1.

Study the active and passive forms of the *present simple* and *past simple*:

Present simple
active: **clean(s)** / **see(s)** etc.   Somebody **cleans** this room every day.

passive: **am/is/are** + **cleaned/seen** etc.   This room **is cleaned** every day.

- ☐ Many accidents **are caused** by careless driving.
- ☐ **I'm not** often **invited** to parties.
- ☐ How **is** this word **pronounced**?

Past simple
active: **cleaned/saw** etc.   Somebody **cleaned** this room yesterday.

passive: **was/were** + **cleaned/seen** etc.   This room **was cleaned** yesterday.

- ☐ We **were woken** up by a loud noise during the night.
- ☐ 'Did you go to the party?' 'No, I **wasn't invited**.'
- ☐ How much money **was stolen** in the robbery?

Unit 42 - Passive 1 - exercises

42.1 Complete the sentences using one of these verbs in the correct form, present or past:

~~cause~~   damage   hold   invite   make
overtake   show   surround   translate   write

1 Many accidents __are caused__ by dangerous driving.
2 Cheese _____ from milk.
3 The roof of the building _____ in a storm a few days ago.
4 You _____ to the wedding. Why didn't you go?
5 A cinema is a place where films _____ .
6 In the United States, elections for president _____ every four years.
7 Originally the book _____ in Spanish, and a few years ago it _____ into English.
8 Although we were driving quite fast, we _____ by a lot of other cars.
9 You can't see the house from the road. It _____ by trees.

42.2 Write questions using the passive. Some are present and some are past.

1 Ask about glass. (how / make?) __How is glass made?__
2 Ask about television. (when / invent?) _____
3 Ask about mountains. (how / form?) _____
4 Ask about Pluto (*the planet*). (when / discover?) _____
5 Ask about silver. (what / use for?) _____

42.3 Put the verb into the correct form, present simple or past simple, active or passive.

1 It's a big factory. Five hundred people __are employed__ (employ) there.
2 __Did somebody clean__ (somebody / clean) this room yesterday?
3 Water _____ (cover) most of the earth's surface.
4 How much of the earth's surface _____ (cover) by water?
5 The park gates _____ (lock) at 6.30 p.m. every evening.
6 The letter _____ (post) a week ago and it _____ (arrive) yesterday.
7 The boat hit a rock and _____ (sink) quickly. Fortunately everybody _____ (rescue).
8 Richard's parents _____ (die) when he was very young. He and his sister _____ (bring up) by their grandparents.
9 I was born in London, but I _____ (grow up) in Canada.
10 While I was on holiday, my camera _____ (steal) from my hotel room.
11 While I was on holiday, my camera _____ (disappear) from my hotel room.
12 Why _____ (Sue / resign) from her job? Didn't she enjoy it?
13 Why _____ (Bill / sack) from his job? What did he do wrong?
14 The company is not independent. It _____ (own) by a much larger company.
15 I saw an accident last night. Somebody _____ (call) an ambulance but nobody _____ (injure), so the ambulance _____ (not / need).
16 Where _____ (these photographs / take)? In London? _____ (you / take) them, or somebody else?
17 Sometimes it's quite noisy living here, but it's not a problem for me – I _____ (not / bother) by it.

42.4 Rewrite these sentences. Instead of using **somebody**, **they**, **people** etc., write a passive sentence.

1 Somebody cleans the room every day.   __The room is cleaned every day.__
2 They cancelled all flights because of fog.   All _____
3 People don't use this road much.   _____
4 Somebody accused me of stealing money.   I _____
5 How do people learn languages?   How _____
6 Somebody warned us not to go out alone.   _____

85

Unit 43 - Passive 2 - lesson

Study the following active and passive forms:

Infinitive
active: (to) **do/clean/see** etc.   Somebody **will clean** the room later.

passive: (to) **be + done/cleaned/seen** etc.   The room **will be cleaned** later.

- □ The situation is serious. Something must **be done** before it's too late.
- □ A mystery is something that can't **be explained**.
- □ The music was very loud and could **be heard** from a long way away.
- □ A new supermarket is going **to be built** next year.
- □ Please go away. I want **to be left** alone.

Perfect infinitive
active: (to) **have + done/cleaned/seen** etc.   Somebody **should have cleaned** the room .

passive: (to) **have been + done/cleaned/seen** etc.   The room **should have been cleaned**.

- □ I haven't received the letter yet. It might **have been sent** to the wrong address.
- □ If you hadn't left the car unlocked, it wouldn't **have been stolen**.
- □ There were some problems at first, but they seem **to have been solved**.

Present perfect
active: **have/has + done** etc.   The room looks nice. Somebody **has cleaned** it .

passive: **have/has been + done** etc.   The room looks nice. It **has been cleaned**.

- □ Have you heard? The concert **has been cancelled**.
- □ **Have** you ever **been bitten** by a dog?
- □ 'Are you going to the party?'   'No, I **haven't been invited**.'

Past perfect
active: **had + done** etc.   The room looked nice. Somebody **had cleaned** it .

passive: **had been + done** etc.   The room looked nice. It **had been cleaned**.

- □ The vegetables didn't taste very good. They **had been cooked** too long.
- □ The car was three years old but **hadn't been used** very much.

Present continuous
active: **am/is/are + (do)ing**   Somebody **is cleaning** the room at the moment.

passive: **am/is/are + being (done)**   The room **is being cleaned** at the moment.

- □ There's somebody walking behind us. I think we **are being followed**.
- □ *(in a shop)* 'Can I help you?'   'No, thank you. I'm **being served**.'

Past continuous
active: **was/were + (do)ing**   Somebody **was cleaning** the room when I arrived.

passive: **was/were + being (done)**   The room **was being cleaned** when I arrived.

- □ There was somebody walking behind us. We **were being followed**.

Unit 43 - Passive 2 - exercises

43.1 What do these words mean? Use it can ... or it can't ... . Use a dictionary if necessary.
If something is
1 washable, *it can be washed* .   4 unusable, ...
2 unbreakable, it ....   5 invisible, ...
3 edible, ...   6 portable, ...

43.2 Complete these sentences with the following verbs (in the correct form):
   arrest   carry   cause   ~~do~~   make   repair   ~~send~~   spend   wake up
Sometimes you need have (might have, should have etc.).
1 The situation is serious. Something must *be done* before it's too late.
2 I haven't received the letter. It might *have been sent* to the wrong address.
3 A decision will not .... until the next meeting.
4 Do you think that more money should .... on education?
5 This road is in very bad condition. It should .... a long time ago.
6 The injured man couldn't walk and had to ....
7 It's not certain how the fire started, but it might .... by an electrical fault.
8 I told the hotel receptionist I wanted to .... at 6.30 the next morning.
9 If you hadn't pushed the policeman, you wouldn't ....

43.3 Rewrite these sentences. Instead of using somebody or they etc., write a passive sentence.
1 Somebody has cleaned the room. *The room has been cleaned.*
2 They have postponed the meeting. The ....
3 Somebody is using the computer at the moment.
   The computer ....
4 I didn't realise that somebody was recording our conversation.
   I didn't realise that ....
5 When we got to the stadium, we found that they had cancelled the game.
   When we got to the stadium, we found that ....
6 They are building a new ring road round the city.
   ....
7 They have built a new hospital near the airport.
   ....

43.4 Make sentences from the words in brackets. Sometimes the verb is active, sometimes passive.
1 There's somebody behind us. (I think / we / follow) *I think we're being followed.*
2 This room looks different. (you / paint / the walls?) *Have you painted the walls?*
3 My car has disappeared. (it / steal!) It ....
4 My umbrella has disappeared. (somebody / take) Somebody ....
5 Sam gets a higher salary now. (he / promote) He ....
6 Ann can't use her office at the moment. (it / redecorate) It ....
7 The photocopier broke down yesterday, but now it's OK. (it / work / again ; it / repair)
   It .... It ....
8 When I went into the room, I saw that the table and chairs were not in the same place.
   (the furniture / move) The ....
9 The man next door disappeared six months ago. (he / not / see / since then)
   He ....
10 I wonder how Jane is these days. (I / not / see / for ages)
   I ....
11 A friend of mine was mugged on his way home a few nights ago. (you / ever / mug?)
   ....

Unit 44 - Passive 3 - lesson

I was offered … / we were given … etc.

Some verbs can have two objects. For example, give:

☐ Somebody gave <u>the police</u> <u>the information</u>. (= Somebody gave the information to the police)

                     object 1   *object 2*

So it is possible to make two passive sentences:

☐ **The police** were given the information. *or*

  The information was given to the police.

Other verbs which can have two objects are:

    ask   offer   pay   show   teach   tell

When we use these verbs in the passive, most often we begin with the *person*:

☐ **I was offered** the job, but I refused it. (= they offered me the job)

☐ **You will be given** plenty of time to decide. (= we will give you plenty of time)

☐ **Have you been shown** the new machine? (= has anybody shown you?)

☐ **The men were paid** £400 to do the work. (= somebody paid the men £400)

I don't like being …

The passive of **doing/seeing** etc. is **being done / being seen** etc. Compare:

active: I don't like **people telling me** what to do.

passive: I don't like **being told** what to do.

☐ I remember **being taken** to the zoo when I was a child.

   (= I remember somebody taking me to the zoo)

☐ Steve hates **being kept** waiting. (= he hates people keeping him waiting)

☐ We managed to climb over the wall without **being seen**. (= without anybody seeing us)

I was born …

We say 'I **was** born …' (*not* I am born):

☐ I **was born** in Chicago.   } *past*

☐ Where **were** you **born**? (*not* Where are you born?)

but

☐ How many babies **are born** every day?   *present*

Get

You can use **get** instead of **be** in the passive:

☐ There was a fight at the party, but nobody **got hurt**. (= nobody **was** hurt)

☐ I don't often **get invited** to parties. (= I'm not often invited)

☐ I'm surprised Liz **didn't get offered** the job. (= Liz **wasn't offered** the job)

You can use **get** only when things *happen*. For example, you cannot use **get** in the following sentences:

☐ Jill **is liked** by everybody. (*not* gets liked – this is not a 'happening')

☐ He was a mystery man. Very little **was known** about him. (*not* got known)

We use **get** mainly in informal spoken English. You can use **be** in all situations.

We also use **get** in the following expressions (which are not passive in meaning):

  get married, get divorced   **get lost** (= not know where you are)

  get dressed (= put on your clothes)   **get changed** (= change your clothes)

Unit 44 - Passive 3 - exercises

44.1 Write these sentences in another way, beginning in the way shown.

1 They didn't give me the information I needed.
I _wasn't given the information I needed._

2 They asked me some difficult questions at the interview.
I ....

3 Linda's colleagues gave her a present when she retired.
Linda ....

4 Nobody told me about the meeting.
I wasn't ....

5 How much will they pay you for your work?
How much will you ....

6 I think they should have offered Tom the job.
I think Tom ....

7 Has anybody shown you what to do?
Have you ....

44.2 Complete the sentences using **being** + the following (in the correct form):

give   invite   ~~keep~~   knock down   stick   treat

1 Steve hates _being kept_ waiting.
2 We went to the party without ....
3 I like giving presents and I also like .... them.
4 It's a busy road and I don't like crossing it. I'm afraid of ....
5 I'm an adult. I don't like .... like a child.
6 You can't do anything about .... in a traffic jam.

44.3 When were they born? Choose five of these people and write a sentence for each.
(Two of them were born in the same year.)

Beethoven	Galileo	Elvis Presley	1452	1869	1929
Agatha Christie	Mahatma Gandhi	Leonardo da Vinci	1564	1890	1935
~~Walt Disney~~	Martin Luther King	William Shakespeare	1770	~~1901~~	

1 _Walt Disney was born in 1901._
2 ....
3 ....
4 ....
5 ....
6 ....
7 And you? I ....

44.4 Complete the sentences using **get/got** + the following verbs (in the correct form):

ask   damage   ~~hurt~~   pay   steal   sting   stop   use

1 There was a fight at the party, but nobody _got hurt_ .
2 Alex .... by a bee while he was sitting in the garden.
3 These tennis courts don't .... very often. Not many people want to play.
4 I used to have a bicycle, but it .... a few months ago.
5 Rachel works hard but doesn't .... very much.
6 Last night I .... by the police as I was driving home. One of the lights on my car wasn't working.
7 Please pack these things very carefully. I don't want them to ....
8 People often want to know what my job is. I often .... that question.

Unit 45 - It is said that... He is said to... He is supposed to... - lesson

Study this example situation:

Henry is very old. Nobody knows exactly how old he is, but:

It is said that he is 108 years old.

or He **is said to be** 108 years old.

Both these sentences mean: 'People say that he is 108 years old.'

You can use these structures with a number of other verbs, especially:

alleged   believed   considered   expected   known   reported   thought   understood

Compare the two structures:

☐ Cathy works very hard.
    It is said that she works 16 hours a day. *or* She **is said to work** 16 hours a day.
☐ The police are looking for a missing boy.
    It is believed that the boy is wearing *or* The boy **is believed to be wearing** a white pullover and blue jeans.   a white pullover and blue jeans.
☐ The strike started three weeks ago.
    It is expected that it will end soon. *or* The strike **is expected to end** soon.
☐ A friend of mine has been arrested.
    It is alleged that he hit a policeman. *or* He **is alleged to have hit** a policeman.
☐ The two houses belong to the same family.
    It is said that there is a secret tunnel *or* There **is said to be** a secret tunnel between them.   between them.

These structures are often used in news reports. For example, in a report about an accident:

☐ **It is reported that** two people were *or* Two people **are reported to have** injured in the explosion.   **been injured** in the explosion.

(Be) supposed to

Sometimes (**it is**) **supposed to** ... = (it is) said to ... :
    ☐ I want to see that film. It's **supposed to be** good. (= it is said to be good)
    ☐ Mark **is supposed to have hit** a policeman, but I don't believe it.

But sometimes **supposed to** has a different meaning. We use **supposed to** to say what is intended, arranged or expected. Often this is different from the real situation:
    ☐ The plan **is supposed to be** a secret, but everybody seems to know about it.
        (= the plan is intended to be a secret)
    ☐ What are you doing at work? You're **supposed to be** on holiday.
        (= you arranged to be on holiday)
    ☐ Our guests **were supposed to come** at 7.30, but they were late.
    ☐ Jane **was supposed to phone** me last night, but she didn't.
    ☐ I'd better hurry. I'm **supposed to be meeting** Chris in ten minutes.

You're **not supposed to** do something = it is not allowed or advisable:
    ☐ You're **not supposed to park** your car here. It's private parking only.
    ☐ Jeff is much better after his illness, but he's still **not supposed to do** any heavy work.

Unit 45 - It is said that... He is said to... He is supposed to... - exercises

45.1 Write these sentences in another way, beginning as shown. Use the <u>underlined</u> word each time.

1 It is <u>expected</u> that the strike will end soon. The strike _is expected to end soon._

2 It is <u>expected</u> that the weather will be good tomorrow.
The weather is ....

3 It is <u>believed</u> that the thieves got in through a window in the roof.
The thieves ....

4 It is <u>reported</u> that many people are homeless after the floods.
Many people ....

5 It is <u>thought</u> that the prisoner escaped by climbing over a wall.
The prisoner ....

6 It is <u>alleged</u> that the man was driving at 110 miles an hour.
The man ....

7 It is <u>reported</u> that the building has been badly damaged by the fire.
The building ....

8 a It is <u>said</u> that the company is losing a lot of money.
The company ....

   b It is <u>believed</u> that the company lost a lot of money last year.
The company ....

   c It is <u>expected</u> that the company will make a loss this year.
The company ....

45.2 There are a lot of rumours about Alan. Here are some of the things people say about him:

1 (Alan speaks ten languages.)   2 (He knows a lot of famous people.)

3 (He is very rich.)   4 (He has twelve children.)   5 (He was an actor when he was younger.)

Alan

Nobody is sure whether these things are true. Write sentences about Alan using **supposed to.**

1 _Alan is supposed to speak ten languages._

2 He ....

3 ....

4 ....

5 ....

45.3 Complete the sentences using **supposed to be** + the following:

on a diet   a flower   my friend   a joke   ~~a secret~~   working

1 Everybody seems to know about the plan, but it _is supposed to be a secret._

2 You shouldn't criticise me all the time. You ....

3 I shouldn't be eating this cake really. I ....

4 I'm sorry for what I said. I was trying to be funny. It ....

5 What's this drawing? Is it a tree? Or maybe it ....

6 You shouldn't be reading the paper now. You ....

45.4 Write sentences with **supposed to** + the following verbs:

arrive   block   ~~park~~   phone   start

Use the negative (**not supposed to**) where necessary.

1 You _'re not supposed to park_ here. It's private parking only.

2 We .... work at 8.15, but we rarely do anything before 8.30.

3 Oh, I .... Helen, but I completely forgot.

4 This door is a fire exit. You .... it.

5 My train .... at 11.30, but it was an hour late.

Unit 46 - Have something done - lesson

Study this example situation:

LISA

The roof of Lisa's house was damaged in a storm. Yesterday a workman came and repaired it.

Lisa **had** the roof **repaired** yesterday.

This means: Lisa arranged for somebody else to repair the roof. She didn't repair it herself.

We use **have something done** to say that we arrange for somebody else to do something for us. Compare:

- Lisa **repaired** the roof. (= she repaired it herself)
  Lisa **had** the roof **repaired**. (= she arranged for somebody else to repair it)
- 'Did you **make** those curtains yourself?' 'Yes, I enjoy making things.'
  'Did you **have** those curtains **made**?' 'No, I made them myself.'

Be careful with word order. The *past participle* (**repaired/cut** etc.) is after the *object*:

have	object	past participle
Lisa **had**	the roof	**repaired** yesterday.
Where did you **have**	your hair	**cut**?
Your hair looks nice. Have you **had**	it	**cut**?
Our neighbour has just **had**	a garage	**built**.
We are **having**	the house	**painted** at the moment.
How often do you **have**	your car	**serviced**?
I think you should **have**	that coat	**cleaned**.
I don't like **having**	my photograph	**taken**.

Get something done

You can also say 'get something done' instead of '**have** something done' (mainly in informal spoken English):

- When are you going to **get the roof repaired**? (= have the roof repaired)
- I think you should **get your hair cut** really short.

Sometimes **have something done** has a different meaning. For example:

- Paul and Karen **had all their money stolen** while they were on holiday.

This does not mean that they arranged for somebody to steal their money. 'They **had all their money stolen**' means only: 'All their money was stolen from them'.

With this meaning, we use **have something done** to say that something happens to somebody or their belongings. Usually what happens is not nice:

- Gary **had** his nose **broken** in a fight. (= his nose was broken)
- Have you ever **had** your passport **stolen**?

Unit 46 - Have something done - exercises

46.1 Tick (✓) the correct sentence, (a) or (b), for each picture.

1	2	3	4
SARAH	BILL	JOHN	SUE
(a) Sarah is cutting her hair.	(a) Bill is cutting his hair.	(a) John is cleaning his shoes.	(a) Sue is taking a photograph.
(b) Sarah is having her hair cut.	(b) Bill is having his hair cut.	(b) John is having his shoes cleaned.	(b) Sue is having her photograph taken.

46.2 Answer the questions using **To have something done**. Choose from the boxes:

~~my car~~	my eyes	my jacket	my watch

clean	repair	~~service~~	test

1 Why did you go to the garage? _To have my car serviced._
2 Why did you go to the cleaner's? To ___
3 Why did you go to the jeweller's? ___
4 Why did you go to the optician's? ___

46.3 Write sentences in the way shown.

1 Lisa didn't repair the roof herself. She _had it repaired._
2 I didn't cut my hair myself. I ___
3 They didn't paint the house themselves. They ___
4 John didn't build that wall himself. ___
5 I didn't deliver the flowers myself. ___

46.4 Use the words in brackets to complete the sentences. Use the structure **have something done**.

1 We _are having the house painted_ (the house / paint) at the moment.
2 I lost my key. I'll have to ___ (another key / make).
3 When was the last time you ___ (your hair / cut)?
4 ___ (you / a newspaper / deliver) to your house every day, or do you go out and buy one?
5 A: What are those workmen doing in your garden?
   B: Oh, we ___ (a garage / build).
6 A: Can I see the photographs you took when you were on holiday?
   B: I'm afraid I ___ (not / the film / develop) yet.
7 This coat is dirty. I must ___ (it / clean).
8 If you want to wear earrings, why don't you ___ (your ears / pierce)?
9 A: I heard your computer wasn't working.
   B: That's right, but it's OK now. I ___ (it / repair).

In these items, use 'have something done' with its second meaning (see Section D).

10 Gary was in a fight last night. He _had his nose broken_ (his nose / break).
11 Did I tell you about Jane? She ___ (her handbag / steal) last week.
12 Did you hear about Pete? He ___ (his car / vandalise) a few nights ago.

Unit 47 - Reported speech 1 (He said that...) - lesson

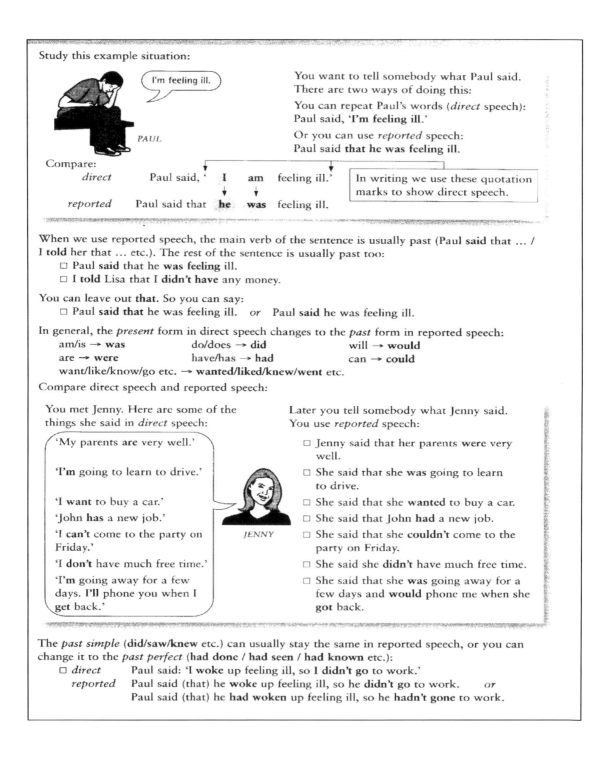

Study this example situation:

I'm feeling ill.

PAUL

You want to tell somebody what Paul said. There are two ways of doing this:

You can repeat Paul's words (*direct* speech):
Paul said, '**I'm feeling ill.**'

Or you can use *reported* speech:
Paul said **that he was feeling ill.**

Compare:

direct	Paul said, '	**I**	**am**	feeling ill.'
reported	Paul said that	**he**	**was**	feeling ill.

In writing we use these quotation marks to show direct speech.

When we use reported speech, the main verb of the sentence is usually past (Paul **said** that ... / I **told** her that ... etc.). The rest of the sentence is usually past too:
- Paul **said** that he **was feeling** ill.
- I **told** Lisa that I **didn't have** any money.

You can leave out **that**. So you can say:
- Paul **said that** he was feeling ill. *or* Paul **said** he was feeling ill.

In general, the *present* form in direct speech changes to the *past* form in reported speech:

am/is → **was**   do/does → **did**   will → **would**
are → **were**   have/has → **had**   can → **could**
want/like/know/go etc. → **wanted/liked/knew/went** etc.

Compare direct speech and reported speech:

You met Jenny. Here are some of the things she said in *direct* speech:

'My parents **are** very well.'

'**I'm** going to learn to drive.'

'I **want** to buy a car.'

'John **has** a new job.'

'I **can't** come to the party on Friday.'

'I **don't** have much free time.'

'**I'm** going away for a few days. **I'll** phone you when I **get** back.'

JENNY

Later you tell somebody what Jenny said. You use *reported* speech:

- Jenny said that her parents **were** very well.
- She said that she **was** going to learn to drive.
- She said that she **wanted** to buy a car.
- She said that John **had** a new job.
- She said that she **couldn't** come to the party on Friday.
- She said she **didn't** have much free time.
- She said that she **was** going away for a few days and **would** phone me when she **got** back.

The *past simple* (did/saw/knew etc.) can usually stay the same in reported speech, or you can change it to the *past perfect* (had done / had seen / had known etc.):
- *direct*   Paul said: 'I **woke** up feeling ill, so I **didn't go** to work.'
  reported   Paul said (that) he **woke** up feeling ill, so he **didn't go** to work.   *or*
              Paul said (that) he **had woken** up feeling ill, so he **hadn't gone** to work.

Unit 47 - Reported speech 1 (He said that...) - exercises

47.1 Yesterday you met a friend of yours, Steve. You hadn't seen him for a long time. Here are some of the things Steve said to you:

1 I'm living in London.

2 My father isn't very well.

3 Rachel and Mark are getting married next month.

4 My sister has had a baby.

5 I don't know what Frank is doing.

6 I saw Helen at a party in June and she seemed fine.

Steve

7 I haven't seen Diane recently.

8 I'm not enjoying my job very much.

9 You can come and stay at my place if you're ever in London.

10 My car was stolen a few days ago.

11 I want to go on holiday, but I can't afford it.

12 I'll tell Chris I saw you.

Later that day you tell another friend what Steve said. Use reported speech.

1 *Steve said that he was living in London.*
2 He said that ....
3 He ....
4 ....
5 ....
6 ....
7 ....
8 ....
9 ....
10 ....
11 ....
12 ....

47.2 Somebody says something to you which is the opposite of what they said earlier. Complete the answers.

1 A: That restaurant is expensive.
   B: Is it? I thought you said *it was cheap* .
2 A: Sue is coming to the party tonight.
   B: Is she? I thought you said she ....
3 A: Sarah likes Paul.
   B: Does she? Last week you said ....
4 A: I know lots of people.
   B: Do you? I thought you said ....
5 A: Jane will be here next week.
   B: Will she? But didn't you say .... ?
6 A: I'm going out this evening.
   B: Are you? But you said ....
7 A: I can speak a little French.
   B: Can you? But earlier you said ....
8 A: I haven't been to the cinema for ages.
   B: Haven't you? I thought you said ....

Unit 48 - Reported speech 2 - lesson

It is not always necessary to change the verb in reported speech. If you report something and the situation *hasn't changed*, you do not need to change the verb to the past:

   □ *direct*   Paul said, 'My new job **is** very interesting.'
      reported   Paul said that his new job **is** very interesting.
                (The situation hasn't changed. His job **is** still interesting.)

   □ *direct*   Helen said, '**I want** to go to New York next year.'
      reported   Helen told me that **she wants** to go to New York next year.
                (Helen still wants to go to New York next year.)

You can also change the verb to the past:
   □ Paul said that his new job **was** very interesting.
   □ Helen told me that she **wanted** to go to New York next year.

But if you are reporting a finished situation, you *must* use a past verb:
   □ Paul left the room suddenly. He said **he had** to go. (*not* has to go)

You need to use a past form when there is a difference
between what was said and what is really true. For example:

You met Sonia a few days ago.
She said: '**Joe is in hospital.**' *(direct speech)*

Later that day you meet Joe in the street. You say:
'I **didn't** expect to see you, Joe. Sonia said you **were** in hospital.'
(*not* 'Sonia said you are in hospital', because clearly he is not)

Say and tell

If you say *who* somebody is talking to, use **tell**:   **TELL SOMEBODY**
   □ Sonia **told me** that you were in hospital. (*not* Sonia said me)
   □ What did you **tell the police**? (*not* say the police)

Otherwise use **say**:   **SAY SOMEBODY**
   □ Sonia **said** that you were in hospital. (*not* Sonia told that …)
   □ What did you **say**?

But you can '**say something to somebody**':
   □ Ann **said** goodbye **to me** and left. (*not* Ann said me goodbye)
   □ What did you **say to the police**?

Tell/ask somebody **to** do something

We also use the infinitive (**to do / to stay** etc.) in reported speech, especially with **tell** and **ask** (for orders and requests):
   □ *direct*   '**Stay** in bed for a few days,' the doctor said to me.
      reported   The doctor **told me to** stay in bed for a few days.
   □ *direct*   '**Don't shout**,' I said to Jim.
      reported   I **told Jim not to** shout.
   □ *direct*   'Please **don't tell** anybody what happened,' Jackie said to me.
      reported   Jackie **asked me not to** tell anybody what (had) happened.

You can also say '**Somebody said (not) to** do something':
   □ Jackie **said** not **to tell** anyone. (*but not* Jackie said me)

Unit 48 - Reported speech 2 - exercises

48.1 Here are some things that Sarah said to you:

I've never been to the United States.

I don't have any brothers or sisters.

I can't drive.

I don't like fish.

Jane has a very well-paid job.

I'm working tomorrow evening.

Jane is a friend of mine.

Dave is lazy.

But later Sarah says something different to you. What do you say?

	Sarah	You
1	Dave works very hard.	*But you said he was lazy.*
2	Let's have fish for dinner.	But ....
3	I'm going to buy a car.	....
4	Jane is always short of money.	....
5	My sister lives in Paris.	....
6	I think New York is a great place.	....
7	Let's go out tomorrow evening.	....
8	I've never spoken to Jane.	....

48.2 Complete the sentences with say or tell (in the correct form). Use only one word each time.

1 Ann __*said*__ goodbye to me and left.
2 .... us about your holiday. Did you have a nice time?
3 Don't just stand there! .... something!
4 I wonder where Sue is. She .... she would be here at 8 o'clock.
5 Dan .... me that he was bored with his job.
6 The doctor .... that I should rest for at least a week.
7 Don't .... anybody what I .... It's a secret just between us.
8 'Did she .... you what happened?' 'No, she didn't .... anything to me.'
9 Gary couldn't help me. He .... me to ask Caroline.
10 Gary couldn't help me. He .... to ask Caroline.

48.3 The following sentences are direct speech:

Don't wait for me if I'm late.

Mind your own business.

Don't worry, Sue.

Please slow down!

Can you open your bag, please?

Could you get a newspaper?

Hurry up!

Will you marry me?

Do you think you could give me a hand, Tom?

Now choose one of these to complete each of the sentences below. Use <u>reported</u> speech.

1 Bill was taking a long time to get ready, so I *told him to hurry up* .
2 Sarah was driving too fast, so I asked ....
3 Sue was nervous about the situation. I told ....
4 I couldn't move the piano alone, so I ....
5 The customs officer looked at me suspiciously and ....
6 Tom was going to the shop, so I ....
7 The man started asking me personal questions, so I ....
8 John was very much in love with Mary, so he ....
9 I didn't want to delay Helen, so I ....

Unit 49 - Questions 1 - lesson

In questions we usually put the subject after the first verb:

   subject + verb   *verb + subject*

Tom	will	→	will	Tom?
you	have	→	have	you?
the house	was	→	was	the house?

☐ **Will Tom** be here tomorrow?
☐ **Have you** been working hard?
☐ When **was the house** built?

Remember that the subject comes after the *first* verb:
   ☐ **Is Catherine** working today? (*not* Is working Catherine)

In *present simple* questions, we use **do/does**:

you	live	→	**do**	you live?
the film	begins	→	**does**	the film begin?

☐ **Do you** li e near here?
☐ What time **does the film begin**?

In *past simple* questions, we use **did**:

you	sold	→	**did**	you sell?
the train	stopped	→	**did**	the train stop?

☐ **Did you sell** your car?
☐ Why **did the train stop**?

But do not use **do/does/did** if **who/what** etc. is the subject of the sentence. Compare:

who *object*

Emma telephoned somebody .

┌──── *object* ────
Who did Emma telephone?

who *subject*

Somebody telephoned Emma.

subject

Who telephoned Emma?

In these examples, **who/what** etc. is the *subject*:
   ☐ **Who wants** something to eat? (*not* Who does want)
   ☐ **What happened** to you last night? (*not* What did happen)
   ☐ **How many people came** to the meeting? (*not* did come)
   ☐ **Which bus goes** to the centre? (*not* does go)

Note the position of prepositions in questions beginning **Who/What/Which/Where** ... ?:
   ☐ **Who** do you want to speak **to**?   ☐ **What** was the weather like yesterday?
   ☐ **Which** job has Ann applied **for**?   ☐ **Where** are you **from**?

You can use *preposition* + **whom** in formal style:
   ☐ **To whom** do you wish to speak?

Isn't it ... ? / Didn't you ... ? etc. (negative questions)

We use negative questions especially to show surprise:
   ☐ **Didn't you** hear the doorbell? I rang it three times.
or when we expect the listener to agree with us:
   ☐ '**Haven't we** met somewhere before?' 'Yes, I think we have.'

Note the meaning of **yes** and **no** in answers to negative questions:
   ☐ **Don't you** want to go to the party? { **Yes.** (= Yes, I want to go) / **No.** (= No, I don't want to go) }

Note the word order in negative questions beginning **Why** ... ?:
   ☐ **Why don't we** go out for a meal tonight? (*not* Why we don't go)
   ☐ **Why wasn't Mary** at work yesterday? (*not* Why Mary wasn't)

Unit 49 - Questions 1 - exercises

49.1 Ask Joe questions. (Look at his answers before you write the questions.)

1	(where / live?) Where do you live?	In Manchester.
2	(born there?)	No, I was born in London.
3	(married?)	Yes.
4	(how long / married?)	17 years.
5	(children?)	Yes, two boys.
6	(how old / they?)	12 and 15.
7	(what / do?)	I'm a journalist.
8	(what / wife / do?)	She's a doctor.

Joe

49.2 Make questions with who or what.

1	Somebody hit me.	Who hit you?
2	I hit somebody.	Who did you hit?
3	Somebody paid the bill.	Who
4	Something happened.	What
5	Diane said something.	
6	This book belongs to somebody.	
7	Somebody lives in that house.	
8	I fell over something.	
9	Something fell on the floor.	
10	This word means something.	
11	I borrowed the money from somebody.	
12	I'm worried about something.	

49.3 Put the words in brackets in the correct order. All the sentences are questions.

1 (when / was / built / this house) When was this house built?
2 (how / cheese / is / made)
3 (when / invented / the computer / was)
4 (why / Sue / working / isn't / today)
5 (what time / coming / your friends / are)
6 (why / was / cancelled / the concert)
7 (where / your mother / was / born)
8 (why / you / to the party / didn't / come)
9 (how / the accident / did / happen)
10 (why / this machine / doesn't / work)

49.4 Write negative questions from the words in brackets. In each situation you are surprised.

1 A: We won't see Liz this evening.
   B: Why not? (she / not / come / to the party?) Isn't she coming to the party?
2 A: I hope we don't meet David tonight.
   B: Why? (you / not / like / him?)
3 A: Don't go and see that film.
   B: Why not? (it / not / good?)
4 A: I'll have to borrow some money.
   B: Why? (you / not / have / any?)

Unit 50 - Questions 2 - lesson

Do you know where … ? / I don't know why … / Could you tell me what … ? etc.

We say: Where **has** Tom gone?

but   **Do you know** where Tom **has** gone?   (*not* Do you know where has Tom gone?)

When the question (**Where has Tom gone?**) is part of a longer sentence (**Do you know** … ? / **I don't know** … / **Can you tell me** … ? etc.), the word order changes. We say:

☐ What time **is it**?	*but*	**Do you know** what time it **is**?
☐ Who **are those people**?		**I don't know** who those people **are**.
☐ Where **can I** find Linda?		**Can you tell me** where I **can** find Linda?
☐ How much **will it** cost?		**Do you have any idea** how much it **will** cost?

Be careful with **do/does/did** questions. We say:

☐ What time **does the film begin**?	*but*	**Do you know** what time **the film begins**?
		(*not* does the film begin)
☐ What **do you mean**?		**Please explain** what **you mean**.
☐ Why **did she leave** early?		**I wonder** why **she left** early.

Use **if** or **whether** where there is no other question word (**what, why** etc.):

☐ **Did anybody** see you?	*but*	**Do you know if** anybody **saw** you?
		or … **whether** anybody **saw** you?

He asked me where … (reported questions)

The same changes in word order happen in reported questions. Compare:

☐ *direct*   The police officer said to us, 'Where **are you going** ?'

   reported   The police officer asked us where **we were going** .

☐ *direct*   Clare said, 'What time **do the banks close** ?'

   reported   Clare wanted to know what time **the banks closed** .

In reported speech the verb usually changes to the past (**were, closed** etc.). See Unit 47.

Study these examples. You had an interview for a job and these were some of the questions the interviewer asked you:

Are you willing to travel?

Why **did you apply** for the job?

What **do you do** in your spare time?

Can you speak any foreign languages?

How long **have you been** working in your present job?

Do you have a driving licence?

Later you tell a friend what the interviewer asked you. You use *reported* speech:

☐ She asked if (*or* whether) **I was** willing to travel.
☐ She wanted to know what **I did** in my spare time.
☐ She asked how long **I had** been working in my present job.
☐ She asked why **I had** applied for the job. (*or* … why **I applied**)
☐ She wanted to know if (*or* whether) **I could** speak any foreign languages.
☐ She asked if (*or* whether) **I had** a driving licence.

Unit 50 - Questions 2 - exercises

50.1 Make a new sentence from the question in brackets.
1 (Where has Tom gone?) Do you know .....where Tom has gone?.....
2 (Where is the post office?) Could you tell me where ....
3 (What's the time?) I wonder ....
4 (What does this word mean?) I want to know ....
5 (What time did they leave?) Do you know ....
6 (Is Sue going out tonight?) I don't know ....
7 (Where does Caroline live?) Do you have any idea ....
8 (Where did I park the car?) I can't remember ....
9 (Is there a bank near here?) Can you tell me ....
10 (What do you want?) Tell me ....
11 (Why didn't Kate come to the party?) I don't know ....
12 (How much does it cost to park here?) Do you know ....
13 (Who is that woman?) I have no idea ....
14 (Did Liz get my letter?) Do you know ....
15 (How far is it to the airport?) Can you tell me ....

50.2 You are making a phone call. You want to speak to Sue, but she isn't there. Somebody else answers the phone. You want to know three things:
(1) Where has she gone? (2) When will she be back? and (3) Did she go out alone?
Complete the conversation:
A: Do you know where .... ? (1)
B: Sorry, I've got no idea.
A: Never mind. I don't suppose you know .... (2)
B: No, I'm afraid not.
A: One more thing. Do you happen to know .... ? (3)
B: I'm afraid I didn't see her go out.
A: OK. Well, thank you anyway. Goodbye.

50.3 You have been away for a while and have just come back to your home town. You meet Tony, a friend of yours. He asks you a lot of questions:

1 (How are you?)   5 (Why did you come back?)   6 (Where are you living?)

2 (Where have you been?)   7 (Are you glad to be back?)

3 (How long have you been back?)   8 (Do you have any plans to go away again?)

4 (What are you doing now?)   Tony   9 (Can you lend me some money?)

Now you tell another friend what Tony asked you. Use reported speech.
1 ....He asked me how I was.....
2 He asked me ....
3 He ....
4 ....
5 ....
6 ....
7 ....
8 ....
9 ....

Unit 51 - Auxiliary verbs and I think so/I hope so etc - lesson

In each of these sentences there is an auxiliary verb and a main verb:

I	have	lost	my keys.
She	can't	come	to the party.
The hotel	was	built	ten years ago.
Where	do you	live?	

In these examples **have/can't/was/do** are auxiliary (= helping) verbs.

You can use an auxiliary verb when you don't want to repeat something:
- □ 'Have you locked the door?' 'Yes, I **have**.' (= I have *locked the door*)
- □ George wasn't working, but Janet **was**. (= Janet was *working*)
- □ She could lend me the money, but she **won't**. (= she won't *lend me the money*)

Use **do/does/did** for the present and past simple:
- □ 'Do you like onions?' 'Yes, I **do**.' (= I *like onions*)
- □ 'Does Simon live in London?' 'He **did**, but he **doesn't** any more.'

You can use auxiliary verbs to deny what somebody says (= say it is not true):
- □ 'You're sitting in my place.' 'No, I'**m not**.' (= I'm not *sitting in your place*)
- □ 'You didn't lock the door before you left.' 'Yes, I **did**.' (= I *locked the door*)

We use **have you?** / **isn't she?** / **do they?** etc. to show interest in what somebody has said or to show surprise:
- □ 'I've just seen Simon.' 'Oh, **have you**? How is he?'
- □ 'Liz isn't very well today.' 'Oh, **isn't she**? What's wrong with her?'
- □ 'It rained every day during our holiday.' '**Did it**? What a pity!'
- □ 'Jim and Nora are getting married.' '**Are they**? Really?'

We use auxiliary verbs with **so** and **neither**:
- □ 'I'm feeling tired.' '**So am I**.' (= I'm feeling tired too)
- □ 'I never read newspapers.' '**Neither do I**.' (= I never read newspapers either)
- □ Sue hasn't got a car and **neither has Martin**.

Note the word order after **so** and **neither** (verb before subject):
- □ I passed the exam and **so did Paul**. (*not* so Paul did)

Instead of **neither**, you can use **nor**. You can also use **not … either**:
- □ 'I don't know.' '**Neither do I**.' *or* '**Nor do I**.' *or* 'I **don't either**.'

I think so / I hope so etc.

After some verbs you can use **so** when you don't want to repeat something:
- □ 'Are those people English?' '**I think so**.' (= I think *they are English*)
- □ 'Will you be at home this evening?' '**I expect so**. (= I expect *I'll be at home* …)
- □ 'Do you think Kate has been invited to the party?' '**I suppose so**.'

In the same way we say: **I hope so, I guess so** and **I'm afraid so**.

The usual negative forms are:

I think so / I expect so	→	I don't think so / I don't expect so
I hope so / I'm afraid so / I guess so	→	I hope not / I'm afraid not / I guess not
I suppose so	→	I don't suppose so *or* I suppose not

- □ 'Is that woman American?' '**I think so. / I don't think so**.'
- □ 'Do you think it will rain?' '**I hope so. / I hope not**.' (*not* I don't hope so)

Unit 51 - Auxiliary verbs and I think so/I hope so etc - exercises

51.1 Complete each sentence with an auxiliary verb (**do/was/could** etc.). Sometimes the verb must be negative (**don't/wasn't** etc.).

1 I wasn't tired, but my friends ___were___ .
2 I like hot weather, but Ann _____ .
3 'Is Colin here?'   'He _____ five minutes ago, but I think he's gone home now.'
4 Liz said she might phone later this evening, but I don't think she _____ .
5 'Are you and Chris coming to the party?'   'I _____ , but Chris _____ .'
6 I don't know whether to apply for the job or not. Do you think I _____ ?
7 'Please don't tell anybody what I said.'   'Don't worry. I _____ .'
8 'You never listen to me.'   'Yes, I _____ !'
9 'Can you play a musical instrument?'   'No, but I wish I _____ .'
10 'Please help me.'   'I'm sorry. I _____ if I _____ , but I _____ .'

51.2 You never agree with Sue. Answer in the way shown.

1   I'm hungry.   Are you? I'm not.
2   I'm not tired.   Aren't you? I am.
3   I like football.   _____
4   I didn't enjoy the film.   _____
5   I've never been to Australia.   _____   You
6   I thought the exam was easy.   _____

Sue

51.3 You are talking to Tina. If you're in the same position as Tina, reply with So ... or Neither ... as in the first example. Otherwise, ask questions as in the second example.

1   I'm feeling tired.   So am I.
2   I work hard.   Do you? What do you do?
3   I watched television last night.   _____
4   I won't be at home tomorrow.   _____
5   I like reading. I read a lot.   _____   You
6   I'd like to live somewhere else.   _____
7   I can't go out tonight.   _____

Tina

51.4 In these conversations, you are B. Read the information in brackets and then answer with **I think so, I hope not** etc.

1 (You don't like rain.)
  A: Do you think it will rain?   B: (hope) ___I hope not.___
2 (You need more money quickly.)
  A: Do you think you'll get a pay rise soon?   B: (hope) _____
3 (You think Diane will probably get the job that she applied for.)
  A: Do you think Diane will get the job?   B: (expect) _____
4 (You're not sure whether Barbara is married – probably not.)
  A: Is Barbara married?   B: (think) _____
5 (You are the receptionist at a hotel. The hotel is full.)
  A: Have you got a room for tonight?   B: (afraid) _____
6 (You're at a party. You have to leave early.)
  A: Do you have to leave already?   B: (afraid) _____
7 (Ann normally works every day, Monday to Friday. Tomorrow is Wednesday.)
  A: Is Ann working tomorrow?   B: (suppose) _____
8 (You are going to a party. You can't stand John.)
  A: Do you think John will be at the party?   B: (hope) _____
9 (You're not sure what time the concert is – probably 7.30.)
  A: Is the concert at 7.30?   B: (think) _____

103

Unit 52 - Question tags (do you? isn't it? etc.) - lesson

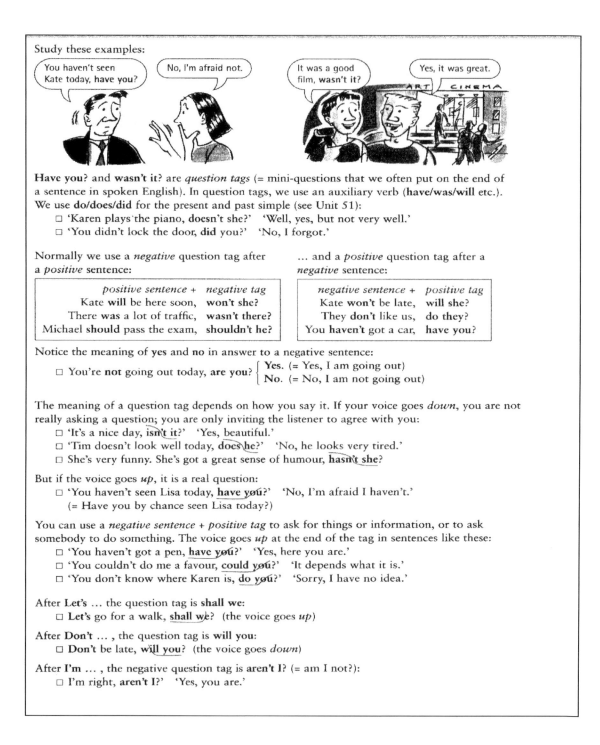

Study these examples:

> You haven't seen Kate today, **have you?**

> No, I'm afraid not.

> It was a good film, **wasn't it?**

> Yes, it was great.

Have you? and **wasn't it?** are *question tags* (= mini-questions that we often put on the end of a sentence in spoken English). In question tags, we use an auxiliary verb (**have/was/will** etc.). We use **do/does/did** for the present and past simple (see Unit 51):

    □ 'Karen plays the piano, **doesn't she?**' 'Well, yes, but not very well.'
    □ 'You didn't lock the door, **did you?**' 'No, I forgot.'

Normally we use a *negative* question tag after a *positive* sentence:

... and a *positive* question tag after a *negative* sentence:

positive sentence +	*negative tag*
Kate **will** be here soon,	**won't she?**
There **was** a lot of traffic,	**wasn't there?**
Michael **should** pass the exam,	**shouldn't he?**

negative sentence +	*positive tag*
Kate **won't** be late,	**will she?**
They **don't** like us,	**do they?**
You **haven't** got a car,	**have you?**

Notice the meaning of **yes** and **no** in answer to a negative sentence:

    □ You're **not** going out today, **are you?** { **Yes.** (= Yes, I am going out)
                                      { **No.** (= No, I am not going out)

The meaning of a question tag depends on how you say it. If your voice goes *down*, you are not really asking a question; you are only inviting the listener to agree with you:

    □ 'It's a nice day, **isn't it?**' 'Yes, beautiful.'
    □ 'Tim doesn't look well today, **does he?**' 'No, he looks very tired.'
    □ She's very funny. She's got a great sense of humour, **hasn't she?**

But if the voice goes *up*, it is a real question:

    □ 'You haven't seen Lisa today, **have you?**' 'No, I'm afraid I haven't.'
       (= Have you by chance seen Lisa today?)

You can use a *negative sentence + positive tag* to ask for things or information, or to ask somebody to do something. The voice goes *up* at the end of the tag in sentences like these:

    □ 'You haven't got a pen, **have you?**' 'Yes, here you are.'
    □ 'You couldn't do me a favour, **could you?**' 'It depends what it is.'
    □ 'You don't know where Karen is, **do you?**' 'Sorry, I have no idea.'

After **Let's** ... the question tag is **shall we:**

    □ **Let's** go for a walk, **shall we?** (the voice goes *up*)

After **Don't** ... , the question tag is **will you:**

    □ **Don't** be late, **will you?** (the voice goes *down*)

After **I'm** ... , the negative question tag is **aren't I?** (= am I not?):

    □ I'm right, **aren't I?**' 'Yes, you are.'

Unit 52 - Question tags (do you? isn't it? etc.) - exercises

52.1 Put a question tag on the end of these sentences.

1	Kate won't be late, _will she_ ?	No, she's never late.
2	You're tired, _aren't you_ ?	Yes, a little.
3	You've got a camera, _____ ?	Yes, I've got two actually.
4	You weren't listening, _____ ?	Yes, I was!
5	Sue doesn't know Ann, _____ ?	No, they've never met.
6	Jack's on holiday, _____ ?	Yes, he's in Portugal.
7	Kate's applied for the job, _____ ?	Yes, but she won't get it.
8	You can speak German, _____ ?	Yes, but not very fluently.
9	He won't mind if I use his phone, _____ ?	No, of course he won't.
10	There are a lot of people here, _____ ?	Yes, more than I expected.
11	Let's go out tonight, _____ ?	Yes, that would be great.
12	This isn't very interesting, _____ ?	No, not very.
13	I'm too impatient, _____ ?	Yes, you are sometimes.
14	You wouldn't tell anyone, _____ ?	No, of course not.
15	Helen has lived here a long time, _____ ?	Yes, 20 years.
16	I shouldn't have lost my temper, _____ ?	No, but never mind.
17	He'd never met her before, _____ ?	No, that was the first time.
18	Don't drop that vase, _____ ?	No, don't worry.

52.2 Read the situation and write a sentence with a question tag. In each situation you are asking your friend to agree with you.

1 You look out of the window. The sky is blue and the sun is shining. What do you say to your friend? (nice day) _It's a nice day, isn't it?_

2 You're with a friend outside a restaurant. You're looking at the prices, which are very high. What do you say? (expensive) It _____

3 You and a colleague have just finished a training course. You really enjoyed it. What do you say to your colleague? (great) The course _____

4 Your friend's hair is much shorter than when you last met. What do you say to her/him? (have / your hair / cut) You _____

5 You and a friend are listening to a woman singing. You like her voice very much. What do you say to your friend? (a good voice) She _____

6 You are trying on a jacket in a shop. You look in the mirror and you don't like what you see. What do you say to your friend? (not / look / very good) It _____

7 You and a friend are walking over a small wooden bridge. The bridge is very old and some parts are broken. What do you say? (not / very safe) This bridge _____

52.3 In these situations you are asking for information, asking people to do things etc.

1 You need a pen. Perhaps Jane has got one. Ask her. _Jane, you haven't got a pen, have you?_

2 Joe is just going out. You want him to get some stamps. Ask him. Joe, you _____

3 You're looking for Diane. Perhaps Kate knows where she is. Ask her. Kate, you _____

4 You need a bicycle pump. Perhaps Helen has got one. Ask her. Helen, _____

5 Ann has a car and you need a lift to the station. Perhaps she'll take you. Ask her. Ann, _____

6 You're looking for your keys. Perhaps Robert has seen them. Ask him. Robert, _____

105

Unit 53 - Verb + ing - lesson

Look at these examples:
- □ I **enjoy** reading. (*not* I enjoy to read)
- □ Would you **mind** closing the door?
  (*not* mind to close)
- □ Chris **suggested** going to the cinema.
  (*not* suggested to go)

After **enjoy**, **mind** and **suggest**, we use -ing (*not* **to** ...).

Some more verbs that are followed by -ing:

stop	postpone	admit	avoid	imagine
finish	consider	deny	risk	fancy

- □ Suddenly everybody **stopped** talking. There was silence.
- □ I'll do the shopping when I've **finished** cleaning the flat.
- □ He tried to **avoid** answering my question.
- □ I don't **fancy** going out this evening. (= I'm not enthusiastic about it)
- □ Have you ever **considered** going to live in another country?

The negative form is **not -ing**:
- □ When I'm on holiday, I **enjoy not** having to get up early.

We also use -ing after:

give up (= stop)
put off (= postpone)
go on / carry on (= continue)
keep *or* **keep on** (= do something continuously or repeatedly)

- □ I've **given up** reading newspapers. I think it's a waste of time.
- □ Jenny doesn't want to retire. She wants to **go on** working. (*or* ... to **carry on** working.)
- □ You **keep** interrupting when I'm talking! *or* You **keep on** interrupting ...

With some verbs you can use the structure *verb* + somebody + -ing:
- □ I can't **imagine George** riding a motorbike.
- □ You can't **stop me** doing what I want.
- □ 'Sorry to **keep you** waiting so long.' 'That's all right.'

Note the passive form (**being done/seen/kept** etc.):
- □ I don't **mind being kept** waiting. (= I don't mind **people** keeping me ...)

When you are talking about finished actions, you can say **having done/stolen/said** etc. :
- □ They admitted **having stolen** the money.

But it is not necessary to use **having** (done). You can also say:
- □ They admitted **stealing** the money.
- □ I now regret **saying** (*or* **having said**) what I said.

For **regret**, see Unit 56B.

After some of the verbs on this page (especially **admit/deny/suggest**) you can also use **that** ... :
- □ They **denied that** they had stolen the money. (*or* They **denied** stealing ...)
- □ Sam **suggested that** we went to the cinema. (*or* Sam **suggested** going ...)

Unit 53 - Verb + ing - exercises

53.1 Complete each sentence with one of the following verbs (in the correct form):

answer   apply   be   forget   listen   live   lose   make   read   try   use   write

1 He tried to avoid *answering* my question.
2 Could you please stop .... so much noise?
3 I enjoy .... to music.
4 I considered .... for the job, but in the end I decided against it.
5 Have you finished .... the newspaper yet?
6 We need to change our routine. We can't go on .... like this.
7 I don't mind you .... the phone as long as you pay for all your calls.
8 My memory is getting worse. I keep .... things.
9 I've put off .... the letter so many times. I really must do it today.
10 What a stupid thing to do! Can you imagine anybody .... so stupid?
11 I've given up .... to lose weight – it's impossible.
12 If you invest your money on the stock market, you risk .... it.

53.2 Complete the sentences for each situation using –ing.

1 What shall we do? / We could go to the zoo.   She suggested *going to the zoo* .

2 Do you want to play tennis? / No, not really.   He didn't fancy ....

3 You were driving too fast. / Yes, it's true. Sorry!   She admitted ....

4 Why don't we go for a swim? / Good idea!   She suggested ....

5 You broke the CD player. / No, I didn't!   He denied ....

6 Can you wait a few minutes? / Sure, no problem.   They didn't mind ....

53.3 Complete the sentences so that they mean the same as the first sentence. Use –ing.

1 I can do what I want and you can't stop me.
   You *can't stop me doing what I want* .
2 It's not a good idea to travel during the rush hour.
   It's better to avoid ....
3 Shall we paint the kitchen next weekend instead of this weekend?
   Shall we postpone .... until .... ?
4 Could you turn the radio down, please?
   Would you mind .... ?
5 Please don't interrupt me all the time.
   Would you mind .... ?

53.4 Use your own ideas to complete these sentences. Use –ing.

1 She's a very interesting person. I always enjoy *talking to her* .
2 I'm not feeling very well. I don't fancy ....
3 I'm afraid there aren't any chairs. I hope you don't mind ....
4 It was a beautiful day, so I suggested ....
5 It was very funny. I couldn't stop ....
6 My car isn't very reliable. It keeps ....

Unit 54 - Verb + to... - lesson

offer	decide	hope	deserve	promise
agree	plan	manage	afford	threaten
refuse	arrange	fail	forget	learn

After these verbs you can use **to** ... (*infinitive*):
- □ It was late, so we **decided to take** a taxi home.
- □ Simon was in a difficult situation, so I **agreed to help** him.
- □ How old were you when you **learnt to drive**? (*or* learnt **how** to drive)
- □ I waved to Karen but **failed to attract** her attention.

The negative is **not to** ... :
- □ We **decided not to go** out because of the weather.
- □ I **promised not to be** late.

After some verbs **to** ... is not possible. For example, **enjoy/think/suggest**:
- □ I **enjoy reading**. (*not* enjoy to read)
- □ Tom **suggested going** to the cinema. (*not* suggested to go)
- □ Are you **thinking of** buying a car? (*not* thinking to buy)

For verb + **-ing**, see Unit 53. For verb + preposition + **-ing**, see Unit 62.

We also use **to** ... after:

seem   appear   tend   pretend   claim

For example:
- □ They **seem to have** plenty of money.
- □ I like Dan, but I think he **tends to talk** too much.
- □ Ann **pretended not to see** me when she passed me in the street.

There is also a *continuous* infinitive (**to be** doing) and a *perfect* infinitive (**to have** done):
- □ I **pretended to be reading** the newspaper. (= I pretended that I **was** reading)
- □ You **seem to have lost** weight. (= it seems that you **have lost** weight)
- □ Martin **seems to be enjoying** his new job. (= it seems that he **is** enjoying it)

After **dare** you can use the infinitive with or without **to**:
- □ I wouldn't **dare to tell** him.   *or*   I wouldn't **dare tell** him.

But after **dare not** (*or* **daren't**), you must use the infinitive without **to**:
- □ I **daren't tell** him what happened. (*not* I daren't to tell him)

After some verbs you can use a question word (**what/whether/how** etc.) + **to** ... . We use this structure especially after:

ask   decide   know   remember   forget   explain   learn   understand   wonder

We asked	how	to get	to the station.
Have you **decided**	where	to go	for your holidays?
I don't **know**	whether	to apply	for the job or not.
Do you **understand**	what	to do?	

Also **show/tell/ask/advise/teach** somebody **what/how/where** to do something:
- □ Can somebody **show me how to change** the film in this camera?
- □ Ask Jack. He'll **tell you what to do**.

Unit 54 - Verb + to... - exercises

54.1 Complete the sentences for these situations.

1 Shall we get married? / Yes, let's. They decided _to get_
   married .

2 Please help me. / OK. She agreed _____
   _____ .

3 Can I carry your bag for you? / No, thanks. I can manage. He offered _____
   _____ .

4 Let's meet at 8 o'clock. / OK, fine. They arranged _____
   _____ .

5 What's your name? / I'm not going to tell you. She refused _____
   _____ .

6 Please don't tell anyone. / I won't. I promise. She promised _____
   _____ .

54.2 Complete each sentence with a suitable verb.

1 Don't forget _to post_ the letter I gave you.
2 There was a lot of traffic, but we managed _____ to the airport in time.
3 Jill has decided not _____ a car.
4 We've got a new computer in our office. I haven't learnt _____ it yet.
5 Karen failed _____ a good impression at the job interview.
6 We were all afraid to speak. Nobody dared _____ anything.

54.3 Put the verb into the correct form, to ... or –ing. (See Unit 53 for verbs + –ing.)

1 When I'm tired, I enjoy _watching_ television. It's relaxing. (watch)
2 It was a nice day, so we decided _____ for a walk. (go)
3 It's a nice day. Does anyone fancy _____ for a walk? (go)
4 I'm not in a hurry. I don't mind _____ . (wait)
5 They don't have much money. They can't afford _____ out very often. (go)
6 I wish that dog would stop _____ . It's driving me mad. (bark)
7 Our neighbour threatened _____ the police if we didn't stop the noise. (call)
8 We were hungry, so I suggested _____ dinner early. (have)
9 Hurry up! I don't want to risk _____ the train. (miss)
10 I'm still looking for a job, but I hope _____ something soon. (find)

54.4 Make a new sentence using the verb in brackets.

1 You've lost weight. (seem) _You seem to have lost weight._
2 Tom is worried about something. (appear) Tom appears _____
3 You know a lot of people. (seem) You _____
4 My English is getting better. (seem) _____
5 That car has broken down. (appear) _____
6 David forgets things. (tend) _____
7 They have solved the problem. (claim) _____

54.5 Complete each sentence using **what/how/whether** + the following verbs:

do ~~get~~ go ride say use

1 Do you know _how to get_ to John's house?
2 Can you show me _____ this washing machine?
3 Would you know _____ if there was a fire in the building?
4 You'll never forget _____ a bicycle once you've learnt.
5 I was really astonished. I didn't know _____ .
6 I've been invited to the party, but I haven't decided _____ or not.

113

Unit 55 - Verb (+ object) + to... - lesson

want	ask	help		would like
expect	beg	mean (= intend)		would prefer

These verbs are followed by **to** ... (*infinitive*). The structure can be:

verb + **to** ...   *or*   *verb* + *object* + **to** ...

- □ We **expected to be** late.
- □ **Would** you **like to go** now?
- □ He doesn't **want to know**.

- □ We **expected Dan to be** late.
- □ Would you like **me to go** now?
- □ He doesn't want **anybody to know**.

Do not say 'want that':
- □ Do you **want me to come** with you? (*not* Do you want that I come)

After **help** you can use the infinitive with or without **to**. So you can say:
- □ Can you help me **to move** this table?   *or*   Can you help me **move** this table?

tell	remind	force	encourage	teach	enable
order	warn	invite	persuade	get (= persuade, arrange for)	

These verbs have the structure *verb* + *object* + **to** ... :
- □ Can you **remind me to phone** Sam tomorrow?
- □ Who **taught you to drive?**
- □ I didn't move the piano by myself. **I got somebody to help** me.
- □ Jim said the switch was dangerous and **warned me not to touch** it.

In the next example, the verb is *passive* (**I was warned** / **we were told** etc.):
- □ **I was warned not to touch** the switch.

You cannot use **suggest** with the structure *verb* + *object* + **to** ... :
- □ Jane **suggested that I should ask** your advice. (*not* Jane suggested me to ask)

After **advise, recommend** and **allow**, two structures are possible. Compare:

verb + **-ing** (without an object)   *verb* + *object* + **to** ...

- □ I wouldn't **advise/recommend** staying in that hotel.
- □ They don't **allow** parking in front of the building.

- □ I wouldn't **advise/recommend anybody to stay** in that hotel.
- □ They don't **allow people to park** in front of the building.

Study these examples with (**be**) **allowed** (*passive*):
- □ **Parking isn't allowed** in front of the building.

- □ **You aren't allowed to park** in front of the building.

Make and **let**

These verbs have the structure *verb* + *object* + *infinitive* (without **to**):
- □ **I made him promise** that he wouldn't tell anybody what happened. (*not* to promise)
- □ Hot weather **makes me feel** tired. (= causes me to feel tired)
- □ Her parents wouldn't **let her go** out alone. (= wouldn't allow her to go out)
- □ **Let me carry** your bag for you.

We say '**make somebody do**' (*not* to do), but the *passive* is '(**be**) **made to do**' (with **to**):
- □ We **were made to wait** for two hours. (= They **made us wait** ...)

114

Unit 55 - Verb (+ object) + to... - exercises

55.1 Complete the questions. Use **do you want me to ... ?** or **would you like me to ... ?** with these verbs (+ any other necessary words):

~~come~~   lend   repeat   show   shut   wait

1 Do you want to go alone, or _do you want me to come with you_ ?
2 Do you have enough money, or do you want _____ ?
3 Shall I leave the window open, or would you _____ ?
4 Do you know how to use the machine, or would _____ ?
5 Did you hear what I said, or do _____ ?
6 Can I go now, or do _____ ?

55.2 Complete the sentences for these situations.

1   Lock the door. / OK.   She told _him to lock the door_ .

2   Why don't you come and stay with us? / That would be nice.   They invited him _____ .

3   Can I use your phone? / No!   She wouldn't let _____ .

4   Be careful. / Don't worry. I will.   She warned _____ .

5   Can you give me a hand? / Sure.   He asked _____ .

55.3 Complete each second sentence so that the meaning is similar to the first sentence.

1 My father said I could use his car.   My father allowed _me to use his car._
2 I was surprised that it rained.   I didn't expect _____
3 Don't stop him doing what he wants.   Let _____
4 Tim looks older when he wears glasses.   Tim's glasses make _____
5 I think you should know the truth.   I want _____
6 Don't let me forget to phone my sister.   Remind _____
7 At first I didn't want to apply for the   Sarah persuaded _____
  job, but Sarah persuaded me.
8 My lawyer said I shouldn't say   My lawyer advised _____
  anything to the police.   _____
9 I was told that I shouldn't believe   I was warned _____
  everything he says.   _____
10 If you've got a car, you are able to get Having a car enables _____
  around more easily.   _____

55.4 Put the verb into the correct form: infinitive (**do/make/eat** etc.), **to** + infinitive, or **–ing**.

1 They don't allow people _to park_ in front of the building. (park)
2 I've never been to Iceland, but I'd like _____ there. (go)
3 I'm in a difficult position. What do you advise me _____ ? (do)
4 The film was very sad. It made me _____ . (cry)
5 Diane's parents always encouraged her _____ hard at school. (study)
6 I don't recommend _____ in that restaurant. The food is terrible. (eat)
7 She said the letter was personal and wouldn't let me _____ it. (read)
8 We are not allowed _____ personal phone calls at work. (make)
9 'I don't think Alex likes me.' 'What makes you _____ that?' (think)

Unit 56 - Verb + ing or to... 1 - lesson

Some verbs are followed by **-ing** and some are followed by **to** ... .

Verbs usually followed by **-ing**:			Verbs usually followed by **to** ... :		
admit	fancy	postpone	afford	fail	offer
avoid	finish	risk	agree	forget	plan
consider	imagine	stop	arrange	hope	promise
deny	keep (on)	suggest	decide	learn	refuse
enjoy	mind		deserve	manage	threaten

For examples, see Unit 53.   For examples, see Unit 54.

Some verbs can be followed by **-ing** or **to** ... with a difference of meaning:

remember

I **remember doing** something = I did it and now I remember this.
You **remember doing** something *after* you have done it.

- I know I locked the door. I clearly **remember locking** it.
  (= I locked it, and now I remember this)
- He could **remember driving** along the road just before the accident, but he couldn't remember the accident itself.

I **remembered to do** something = I remembered that I had to do it, so I did it.
You **remember to do** something *before* you do it.

- I **remembered to lock** the door, but I forgot to shut the windows.
  (= I remembered that I had to lock it, and so I locked it)
- Please **remember to post** the letter.
  (= don't forget to post it)

regret

I **regret doing** something = I did it and now I'm sorry about it:

- I now **regret saying** what I said. I shouldn't have said it.
- It began to get cold and he **regretted not wearing** his coat.

I **regret to say / to tell** you / **to inform** you = I'm sorry that I have to say (etc.):

- *(from a formal letter)* We **regret to inform** you that we cannot offer you the job.

go on

Go on doing something = continue with the same thing:

- The president paused for a moment and then **went on talking**.
- We need to change. We can't **go on living** like this.

Go on to do something = do or say something new:

- After discussing the economy, the president then **went on to talk** about foreign policy.

The following verbs can be followed by **-ing** or **to** ... :
begin   start   continue   intend   bother

So you can say:
- It has **started raining**. *or* It has **started to rain**.
- John **intends buying** a house. *or* John **intends to buy** ...
- Don't **bother locking** the door. *or* Don't **bother to lock** ...

But normally we do not use **-ing** after **-ing**:
- It's **starting to rain**. (*not* It's starting raining)

116

Unit 56 - Verb + ing or to… 1 - exercises

56.1 Put the verb into the correct form, –ing or to … . Sometimes either form is possible.

1 They denied __stealing__ the money. (steal)
2 I don't enjoy _____ very much. (drive)
3 I don't want _____ out tonight. I'm too tired. (go)
4 I can't afford _____ out tonight. I don't have enough money. (go)
5 Has it stopped _____ yet? (rain)
6 Our team was unlucky to lose the game. We deserved _____ . (win)
7 Why do you keep _____ me questions? Can't you leave me alone? (ask)
8 Please stop _____ me questions! (ask)
9 I refuse _____ any more questions. (answer)
10 One of the boys admitted _____ the window. (break)
11 The boy's father promised _____ for the window to be repaired. (pay)
12 If the company continues _____ money, the factory may be closed. (lose)
13 'Does Sarah know about the meeting?' 'No, I forgot _____ her.' (tell)
14 The baby began _____ in the middle of the night. (cry)
15 Julia has been ill, but now she's beginning _____ better. (get)
16 I've enjoyed _____ you. I hope _____ you again soon. (meet, see)

56.2 Here is some information about Tom when he was a child.

1 He was in hospital when he was four.
2 He went to Paris when he was eight.
3 He cried on his first day at school.
4 Once he fell into the river.
5 He said he wanted to be a doctor.
6 Once he was bitten by a dog.

He can still remember 1, 2 and 4. But he can't remember 3, 5 and 6. Write sentences beginning
He can remember … or **He can't remember** … .

1 _He can remember being in hospital when he was four._
2 _____
3 _____
4 _____
5 _____
6 _____

56.3 Complete each sentence with a verb in the correct form, –ing or to … .

1 a Please remember __to lock__ the door when you go out.
  b A: You lent me some money a few months ago.
    B: Did I? Are you sure? I don't remember _____ you any money.
  c A: Did you remember _____ your sister?
    B: Oh no, I completely forgot. I'll phone her tomorrow.
  d When you see Steve, remember _____ him my regards.
  e Someone must have taken my bag. I clearly remember _____ it by the window and now it has gone.
2 a I believe that what I said was fair. I don't regret _____ it.
  b I knew they were in trouble, but I regret _____ I did nothing to help them.
3 a Ben joined the company nine years ago. He became assistant manager after two years, and a few years later he went on _____ manager of the company.
  b I can't go on _____ here any more. I want a different job.
  c When I came into the room, Liz was reading a newspaper. She looked up and said hello, and then went on _____ her newspaper.

Unit 57 - Verb + ing or to... 2 - lesson

Try to ... and try -ing

Try to do = attempt to do, make an effort to do:
- ☐ I was very tired. **I tried to keep** my eyes open, but I couldn't.
- ☐ Please **try to be** quiet when you come home. Everyone will be asleep.

Try also means 'do something as an experiment or test'. For example:
- ☐ These cakes are delicious. You should **try** one. (= you should have one to see if you like it)
- ☐ We couldn't find anywhere to stay. We **tried** every hotel in the town, but they were all full. (= we went to every hotel to see if they had a room)

If **try** (with this meaning) is followed by a verb, we say **try -ing**:
- ☐ A: The photocopier doesn't seem to be working.
    B: **Try pressing** the green button.
    (= press the green button – perhaps this will help to solve the problem)

Compare:
- ☐ I **tried to move** the table, but it was too heavy. (so I couldn't move it)
- ☐ I didn't like the way the furniture was arranged, so I **tried moving** the table to the other side of the room. But it still didn't look right, so I moved it back again.

Need to ... and need -ing

I need to do something = it is necessary for me to do it:
- ☐ I **need to take** more exercise.
- ☐ He **needs to work** harder if he wants to make progress.
- ☐ I don't **need to come** to the meeting, do I?

Something **needs doing** = it needs to be done:
- ☐ The batteries in the radio **need changing**.
    (= they need to be changed)
- ☐ Do you think my jacket **needs cleaning**?
    (= ... needs to be cleaned)
- ☐ It's a difficult problem. It **needs thinking** about very carefully. (= it needs to be thought about)

This room **needs tidying**.

Help and can't help

You can say **help to do** or **help do** (with or without to):
- ☐ Everybody **helped to clean** up after the party.   *or*
    Everybody **helped clean** up ...
- ☐ Can you **help** me **to move** this table?   *or*
    Can you **help** me **move** ...

I can't help doing something = I can't stop myself doing it:
- ☐ I don't like him, but he has a lot of problems. I **can't help feeling** sorry for him.
- ☐ She tried to be serious, but she **couldn't help laughing**.
    (= she couldn't stop herself laughing)
- ☐ I'm sorry I'm so nervous. **I can't help it.**
    (= I can't help **being** nervous)

Unit 57 - Verb + ing or to... 2 - exercises

57.1 Make suggestions. Each time use **try** + one of the following suggestions:

phone his office	move the aerial	~~change the batteries~~
turn it the other way	take an aspirin	

1 The radio isn't working. I wonder what's wrong with it. — Have you _tried changing the batteries?_

2 I can't open the door. The key won't turn. — Try ....

3 The TV picture isn't very good. What can I do about it? — Have you tried ....

4 I can't contact Fred. He's not at home. What shall I do? — Why don't you ....

5 I've got a terrible headache. I wish it would go. — Have you ....

57.2 For each picture, write a sentence with **need(s)** + one of the following verbs:

~~clean~~   cut   empty   paint   tighten

1 This jacket is dirty. _It needs cleaning._ ....
2 The room isn't very nice. ....
3 The grass is very long. It ....
4 The screws are loose. ....
5 The bin is full. ....

57.3 Put the verb into the correct form.

1 a I was very tired. I tried _to keep_ (keep) my eyes open, but I couldn't.
  b I rang the doorbell, but there was no answer. Then I tried .... (knock) on the door, but there was still no answer.
  c We tried .... (put) the fire out but without success. We had to call the fire brigade.
  d Sue needed to borrow some money. She tried .... (ask) Gerry, but he was short of money too.
  e I tried .... (reach) the shelf, but I wasn't tall enough.
  f Please leave me alone. I'm trying .... (concentrate).

2 a I need a change. I need .... (go) away for a while.
  b My grandmother isn't able to look after herself any more. She needs .... (look) after.
  c The windows are dirty. They need .... (clean).
  d Your hair is getting very long. It needs .... (cut).
  e You don't need .... (iron) that shirt. It doesn't need .... (iron).

3 a They were talking very loudly. I couldn't help .... (overhear) what they said.
  b Can you help me .... (get) the dinner ready?
  c He looks so funny. Whenever I see him, I can't help .... (smile).
  d The fine weather helped .... (make) it a very enjoyable holiday.

115

119

Unit 58 - Verb + ing or to... 3 - lesson

Like / love / hate

When you talk about repeated actions, you can use -ing or to ... after these verbs.
So you can say:
- □ Do you **like getting** up early? *or* Do you **like to get** up early?
- □ Stephanie **hates flying**. *or* Stephanie **hates to fly**.
- □ I **love meeting** people. *or* I **love to meet** people.
- □ I don't **like being** kept waiting. *or* ... **like to be** kept waiting.
- □ I don't **like** friends calling me at work. *or* ... friends **to call** me at work.

but

(1) We use **-ing** (*not to ...*) when we talk about a situation that already exists (or existed).
  For example:
  - □ Paul lives in Berlin now. He **likes living** there. (He **likes living** in Berlin = He lives there and he likes it)
  - □ Do you **like being** a student? (You are a student – do you like it?)
  - □ The office I worked in was horrible. I **hated working** there. (I worked there and I hated it)

(2) There is sometimes a difference between **I like to do** and **I like doing**:

  I like doing something = I do it and I enjoy it:
  - □ I **like cleaning** the kitchen. (= I enjoy it.)

  I like to do something = I think it is a good thing to do, but I don't necessarily enjoy it:
  - □ It's not my favourite job, but I **like to clean** the kitchen as often as possible.

Note that **enjoy** and **mind** are always followed by -ing (*not to ...*):
  - □ I **enjoy cleaning** the kitchen. (*not* I enjoy to clean)
  - □ I don't **mind cleaning** the kitchen. (*not* I don't mind to clean)

Would like / would love / would hate / would prefer

Would like / would love etc. are usually followed by **to ...** :
  - □ I'd **like** (= would like) **to go** away for a few days.
  - □ Would you **like to come** to dinner on Friday?
  - □ I wouldn't **like to go** on holiday alone.
  - □ I'd **love to meet** your family.
  - □ Would you **prefer to have** dinner now or later?

Compare **I like** and **I would like** (**I'd like**):
  - □ I **like playing** tennis. / I **like to play** tennis. (= I like it in general)
  - □ I'd **like to play** tennis today. (= I want to play today)

Would mind is always followed by -ing (*not to ...*):
  - □ Would you **mind closing** the door, please?

I would like to have done something = I regret now that I didn't or couldn't do it:
  - □ It's a pity we didn't see Val when we were in London. I **would like to have seen** her again.
  - □ We'd **like to have gone** away, but we were too busy at home.

You can use the same structure after **would love / would hate / would prefer**:
  - □ Poor old David! I **would hate to have been** in his position.
  - □ I'd **love to have gone** to the party, but it was impossible.

Unit 58 - Verb + ing or to... 3 - exercises

58.1 Write sentences about yourself. Say whether you like or don't like these activities. Choose one of these verbs for each sentence:

like / don't like   love   hate   enjoy   don't mind

1 (fly) *I don't like flying.* or *I don't like to fly.*
2 (play cards) ....
3 (be alone) ....
4 (go to museums) ....
5 (cook) ....

58.2 Make sentences from the words in brackets. Use -ing or to ... . Sometimes either form is possible.

1 Paul lives in Berlin now. It's nice. He likes it.
(he / like / live / there) *He likes living there.*
2 Jane is a biology teacher. She likes her job.
(she / like / teach / biology) She ....
3 Joe always carries his camera with him and takes a lot of photographs.
(he / like / take / photographs) ....
4 I used to work in a supermarket. I didn't like it much.
(I / not / like / work / there) ....
5 Rachel is studying medicine. She likes it.
(she / like / study / medicine) ....
6 Dan is famous, but he doesn't like it.
(he / not / like / be / famous) ....
7 Jennifer is a very cautious person. She doesn't take many risks.
(she / not / like / take / risks) ....
8 I don't like surprises.
(I / like / know / things / in advance) ....

58.3 Complete each sentence with a verb in the correct form, -ing or to ... . In one sentence either form is possible.

1 It's good to visit other places – I enjoy ____travelling____ .
2 'Would you like _____ down?' 'No, thanks. I'll stand.'
3 I'm not quite ready yet. Would you mind _____ a little longer?
4 When I was a child, I hated _____ to bed early.
5 When I have to catch a train, I'm always worried that I'll miss it. So I like _____ to the station in plenty of time.
6 I enjoy _____ busy. I don't like it when there's nothing to do.
7 I would love _____ to your wedding, but I'm afraid it isn't possible.
8 I don't like _____ in this part of town. I want to move somewhere else.
9 Do you have a minute? I'd like _____ to you about something.
10 If there's bad news and good news, I like _____ the bad news first.

58.4 Write sentences using would ... to have (done). Use the verbs in brackets.

1 It's a pity I couldn't go to the wedding. (like) *I would like to have gone to the wedding.*
2 It's a pity I didn't see the programme. (like) ....
3 I'm glad I didn't lose my watch. (hate) ....
4 It's a pity I didn't meet your parents. (love) ....
5 I'm glad I wasn't alone. (not / like) ....
6 It's a pity I couldn't travel by train. (prefer) ....

Unit 59 - Prefer and would rather - lesson

Prefer to do and **prefer doing**

You can use 'prefer to (do)' or 'prefer -ing' to say what you prefer in general:
- □ I don't like cities. I **prefer to live** in the country.   *or*   I **prefer living** in the country.

Study the differences in structure after **prefer**. We say:

I prefer	something	to something else.
I prefer	**doing** something	**to doing** something else.
but I prefer	**to do** something	**rather than (do)** something else.

- □ I **prefer** this coat **to** the coat you were wearing yesterday.
- □ I **prefer** driving **to** travelling by train.
- *but* □ I **prefer to drive rather than travel** by train.
- □ Sarah **prefers** to live in the country **rather than (live)** in a city.

Would prefer (I'd prefer ...)

We use **would prefer** to say what somebody wants in a specific situation (not in general):
- □ '**Would** you **prefer** tea or coffee?'   'Coffee, please.'

We say 'would prefer **to do** something' (*not* doing):
- □ 'Shall we go by train?'   'I'd **prefer to drive**.'   (*not* I'd prefer driving)
- □ I'd **prefer to stay** at home tonight **rather than go** to the cinema.

Would rather (I'd rather ...)

Would rather (do) = **would prefer** (to do). We use **would rather** + *infinitive* (without **to**).
Compare:
- □ 'Shall we go by train?' { 'I'd **prefer to drive**.'
                              { 'I'd **rather drive**.' (*not* to drive)
- □ '**Would** you **rather have** tea or coffee?'   'Coffee, please.'

The negative is 'I'd **rather not** (do something)':
- □ I'm tired. I'd **rather not go** out this evening, if you don't mind.
- □ 'Do you want to go out this evening?'   'I'd **rather not**.'

We say '**would rather do** something **than do** something else':
- □ I'd **rather stay** at home tonight **than go** to the cinema.

I'd rather you **did** something

We say '**I'd rather** you **did** something' (*not* I'd rather you do). For example:
- □ 'Shall I stay here?'   'I'd **rather** you **came** with us.'   (= I would prefer this)
- □ 'I'll repair your bike tomorrow, OK?'   'I'd **rather** you **did** it today.'
- □ 'Are you going to tell them what happened?'   'No. I'd **rather** they **didn't** know.'
- □ Shall I tell them, or **would** you **rather** they **didn't** know?

In this structure we use the *past* (**came**, **did** etc.), but the meaning is present *not* past.
Compare:
- □ I'd rather **make** dinner now.
  I'd rather **you made** dinner now.   (*not* I'd rather you make)

I'd rather you **didn't** (do something) = I'd prefer you not to do it:
- □ I'd **rather** you **didn't tell** anyone what I said.
- □ 'Shall I tell Linda what happened?'   'I'd **rather** you **didn't**.'

Unit 59 - Prefer and would rather - exercises

59.1 Which do you prefer? Write sentences using 'I prefer (something) to (something else)'. Put the verb into the correct form where necessary.

1 (drive / travel by train) _I prefer driving to travelling by train._
2 (basketball / football)
   I prefer ....
3 (phone people / send emails)
   I .... to ....
4 (go to the cinema / watch videos at home)
   ....

Now rewrite sentences 3 and 4 using the structure 'I prefer to (do something)'.

5 (1) _I prefer to drive rather than travel by train._
6 (3) I prefer to ....
7 (4) ....

59.2 Write sentences using **I'd prefer** ... and **I'd rather** ... + the following:

eat at home	~~get a taxi~~	go alone	wait a few minutes	listen to some music
stand	go for a swim	~~wait till later~~	think about it for a while	

		(prefer)	_I'd prefer to get a taxi._
1	Shall we walk home?		
2	Do you want to eat now?	(rather)	_I'd rather wait till later._
3	Would you like to watch TV?	(rather)	
4	Do you want to go to a restaurant?	(prefer)	
5	Let's leave now.	(rather)	
6	Shall we play tennis?	(rather)	
7	I think we should decide now.	(prefer)	
8	Would you like to sit down?	(rather)	
9	Do you want me to come with you?	(prefer)	

Now use the same ideas to complete these sentences using **than** and **rather than**.

10 I'd prefer to get a taxi _rather than walk home._
11 I'd prefer to go for a swim ....
12 I'd rather eat at home ....
13 I'd prefer to think about it for a while ....
14 I'd rather listen to some music ....

59.3 Complete the sentences using **would you rather I** ... .

1 Are you going to make dinner or _would you rather I made it_ .... ?
2 Are you going to tell Liz what happened or would you rather .... ?
3 Are you going to do the shopping or .... ?
4 Are you going to phone Diane or .... ?

59.4 Use your own ideas to complete these sentences.

1 'Shall I tell Ann the news?'   'No, I'd rather she _didn't_ know.'
2 Do you want me to go now or would you rather I .... here?
3 Do you want to go out this evening or would you rather .... at home?
4 This is a private letter addressed to me. I'd rather you .... read it.
5 I don't really like these shoes. I'd rather they .... a different colour.
6 A: Do you mind if I turn on the radio?
   B: I'd rather you .... I'm trying to study.

Unit 60 - Prepositions - lesson

If a preposition (**in/for/about** etc.) is followed by a verb, the verb ends in **-ing**:

	preposition	verb (-ing)	
Are you interested	in	working	for us?
I'm not very good	at	learning	languages.
Sue must be fed up	with	studying.	
What are the advantages	of	having	a car?
Thanks very much	for	inviting	me to your party.
How	about	meeting	for lunch tomorrow?
Why don't you go out	instead of	sitting	at home all the time?
Carol went to work	in spite of	feeling	ill.

You can also say 'instead of **somebody** doing something', 'fed up with **people** doing something' etc. :
  □ I'm fed up with **people** telling me what to do.

Note the use of the following prepositions + **-ing**:

before -ing and **after -ing:**

  □ **Before going** out, I phoned Sarah. (*not* Before to go out)
  □ What did you do **after leaving** school?
You can also say '**Before I went** out ...' and '... **after you left** school'.

by -ing (to say *how* something happens):
  □ The burglars got into the house **by breaking** a window and climbing in.
  □ You can improve your English **by reading** more.
  □ She made herself ill **by not eating** properly.
  □ Many accidents are caused **by** people driving too fast.

without -ing:
  □ We ran ten kilometres **without** stopping.
  □ It was a stupid thing to say. I said it **without** thinking.
  □ She needs to work **without** people disturbing her. (*or* ... **without** being disturbed.)
  □ I have enough problems of my own **without** having to worry about yours.

To -ing (look forward **to** doing something etc.)

To is often part of the *infinitive* (**to do** / **to see** etc.):
  □ We decided **to go** out.
  □ Would you like **to meet** for lunch tomorrow?

But **to** is also a *preposition* (like **in/for/about/from** etc.). For example:
  □ We drove from London **to Edinburgh**.
  □ I prefer tea **to coffee**.
  □ Are you looking forward **to the weekend**?

If a preposition is followed by a verb, the verb ends in **-ing**:
  in doing   **about** meeting   **without** stopping (etc.)

So, when **to** is a preposition and it is followed by a verb, you must say **to -ing**:
  □ I prefer driving **to travelling** by train. (*not* to travel)
  □ Are you looking forward **to going** on holiday? (*not* looking forward to go)

Unit 60 - Prepositions - exercises

60.1 Complete the second sentence so that it means the same as the first.

1 Why is it useful to have a car?
What are the advantages of __having a car__ ?

2 I don't intend to apply for the job.
I have no intention of _____ .

3 Helen has a good memory for names.
Helen is good at _____ .

4 Mark won't pass the exam. He has no chance.
Mark has no chance of _____ .

5 Did you get into trouble because you were late?
Did you get into trouble for _____ ?

6 We didn't eat at home. We went to a restaurant instead.
Instead of _____ .

7 We got into the exhibition. We didn't have to queue.
We got into the exhibition without _____ .

8 Our team played well, but we lost the game.
Our team lost the game despite _____ .

60.2 Complete the sentences using **by -ing**. Use the following (with the verb in the correct form):

borrow too much money	~~break a window~~	drive too fast
put some pictures on the walls	stand on a chair	turn a key

1 The burglars got into the house __by breaking a window__ .
2 I was able to reach the top shelf _____ .
3 You start the engine of a car _____ .
4 Kevin got himself into financial trouble _____ .
5 You can put people's lives in danger _____ .
6 We made the room look nicer _____ .

60.3 Complete the sentences with a suitable word. Use only one word each time.

1 We ran ten kilometres without __stopping__ .
2 He left the hotel without _____ his bill.
3 It's a nice morning. How about _____ for a walk?
4 We were able to translate the letter into English without _____ a dictionary.
5 Before _____ to bed, I like to have a hot drink.
6 It was a long journey. I was very tired after _____ on a train for 36 hours.
7 I was annoyed because the decision was made without anybody _____ me.
8 After _____ the same job for ten years, I felt I needed a change.
9 We lost our way because we went straight on instead of _____ left.
10 I like these photographs you took. You're good at _____ photographs.

60.4 For each situation, write a sentence with **I'm (not) looking forward to**.

1 You are going on holiday next week. How do you feel?
__I'm looking forward to going on holiday.__

2 Diane is a good friend of yours and she is coming to visit you soon. So you will see her again soon. How do you feel? I'm _____

3 You are going to the dentist tomorrow. You don't enjoy going to the dentist. How do you feel?
I'm not _____

4 Carol is a student at school. She hates it, but she is leaving school next summer.
How does she feel? _____

5 You've arranged to play tennis tomorrow. You like tennis a lot. How do you feel?
_____

125

Irregular verbs

infinitive	past simple	p.participle	translation
be	was/were	been	
beat	beat	beaten	
become	became	become	
begin	began	begun	
bite	bit	bitten	
blow	blew	blown	
break	broke	broken	
bring	brought	brought	
build	built	built	
burn	burnt/burned	burnt/burned	
buy	bought	bought	
catch	caught	caught	
choose	chose	chosen	
come	came	come	
cost	cost	cost	

cut	cut	cut	
dig	dug	dug	
do	did	done	
draw	drew	drawn	
dream	dreamt/dreamed	dreamt/dreamed	
drink	drank	drunk	
drive	drove	driven	
eat	ate	eaten	
fall	fell	fallen	
feed	fed	fed	
feel	felt	felt	
fight	fought	fought	
find	found	found	
fly	flew	flown	
forget	forgot	forgotten	
forgive	forgave	forgiven	
freeze	froze	frozen	

get	got	got	
give	gave	given	
go	went	gone	
grow	grew	grown	
hang	hanged/hung	hanged/hung	
have	had	had	
hear	heard	heard	
hide	hid	hidden	
hit	hit	hit	
hold	held	held	
hurt	hurt	hurt	
keep	kept	kept	
know	knew	known	
lay	laid	laid	
lead	led	led	
learn	learnt/learned	learnt/learned	
leave	left	left	
lend	lent	lent	

let	let	let	
lie	lay	lain	
lose	lost	lost	
make	made	made	
mean	meant	meant	
meet	met	met	
pay	paid	paid	
put	put	put	
read	read	read	
ride	rode	ridden	
ring	rang	rung	
rise	rose	risen	
run	ran	run	
say	said	said	
see	saw	seen	
sell	sold	sold	
send	sent	sent	
set	set	set	

shake	shook	shaken	
show	showed	shown	
shut	shut	shut	
sing	sang	sung	
sink	sank	sunk	
sit	sat	sat	
sleep	slept	slept	
smell	smelt/smelled	smelt/smelled	
speak	spoke	spoken	
spell	spelt/spelled	spelt/spelled	
spend	spent	spent	
stand	stood	stood	
steal	stole	stolen	
stick	stuck	stuck	
swim	swam	swum	
take	took	taken	
teach	taught	taught	
tear	tore	torn	

tell	told	told	
think	thought	thought	
throw	threw	thrown	
understand	understood	understood	
wake up	woke up	woken up	
wear	wore	worn	
win	won	won	
write	wrote	written	

Printed in Great Britain
by Amazon